THE
SOYBEAN
COOKBOOK

by *Dorothea Van Gundy Jones*

Foreword by Ruth Stout

AN
ARC
BOOK

ARCO PUBLISHING COMPANY, INC.
219 Park Avenue South, New York, N.Y. 10003

An ARC Book
Published by Arco Publishing Company, Inc.
219 Park Avenue South, New York, N.Y. 10003
by arrangement with The Devin-Adair Company, New York.

Fifth ARC Printing, 1973

Library of Congress Catalog Card Number 63-21327
ISBN 0-668-01770-8

Printed in the United States of America

❧ CONTENTS

ᴥ FOREWORD

by Ruth Stout

If you are already a soybean fan, you may think you don't need this book. If you grow this vegetable and eat it when it is green (particularly if you plant the Giant Green variety), you may feel sure that you don't need any recipes because soybeans have such a delicious flavor of their own when you just steam them and season with salt and butter. But leaf through these pages and you will find dozens of recipes which you can hardly wait to try; so many, in fact, that you are likely to feel frustrated, since you can't prepare them all at once, so shut your eyes, play tick-tack-toe and try the one your finger lights on.

And besides the three hundred and fifty recipes, Dorothea Jones tells us everything there is to know, so far, about soybeans, and gives one the distinct feeling that she knows whereof she speaks.

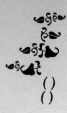

PREFACE
TO THE
FIRST EDITION

Soybeans are perhaps the world's oldest food crop, and for centuries, nutritionally, they have meant meat, milk cheese, bread, and oil to the people of Asia. Economically they have meant gold, a cash crop, something to sell or exchange for other necessities.

We of the Occidental world have also discovered that soybeans are indeed nuggets of gold in our modern civilization. During the last 35 years, they have mushroomed from a little-known forage crop into one of our important cash crops, vital in the fields of agriculture, commerce, nutrition, and industry. Nutritionally soybeans became a vital food for the world at war, and they can be just as important in a world at peace. Industrially they are a challenge to the chemist, for more than two hundred commercial products are made from the beans. Hence soybeans and soybean products are destined to be a vital plus factor in our world of tomorrow.

Food has always been my hobby. When fate, that unseen hand that sometimes guides us to our rightful groove in life, gave me first-hand experience with the miracles of corrective diet, teaching the fundamental facts on nutrition became my goal. I have tried to pass on the message of better eating and living via the platform, the radio, and the printed page. For many years I had the privilege of being on a crossroad of nutrition, working with every phase of the healing art. That was when soybeans were literally thrust upon me. I experimented with them as a food, secured various soy products for special diets, made up recipes, and taught the use and cooking of soybeans when they were practically unknown. At that time soy was eaten because it was soy, regardless of taste or palatability. All this convinced me of the nutritional value of soybeans and their rightful place in our diet. In 1942, when the beans came into the limelight as a war emergency food, a collection of my recipes was published under the title of *150 Ways To Use Soybeans*. In 1945 McGraw-Hill published my complete book on soybeans, their story as well as recipes, called *The Useful Soybean*.

We of the Western Hemisphere know too little of soybeans. Since we have not had to use them as a food, we have not fully appreciated their nutritional merits nor acquired a taste for their flavor. World War II brought them out as an emergency food, an animal protein replacement food. They are just that, and therefore can always be a plus element in our nutrition. We need to know their value and how to use them. Today we need not rely on the bean in its original form, because research has given us palatable soy products to meet every need, taste, and pocketbook.

I believe that proper nutrition and common-sense living are man's best medicine. I also believe that science cannot equal the Master Chemist and that therefore natural foods are better than the refined, even if the latter are enriched. That is why I suggest whole wheat flour, dark sugars, and the like wherever possible. The best selection of natural foods and soy products are found in specialty food stores.

Mildred Lager

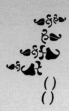

( )
( )

PREFACE
TO THE
REVISED EDITION

Since 1955 research has continued on the soybean, and many new ideas have developed concerning it. New methods have been worked out for removing the too-positive soy flavor in products made from the soybean.

As time goes on, more and more people are discovering the wonderful nutritional value of this king of the legume family. Soybeans are much more popular and widely used today than they were even five years ago.

In the present edition of this book, some recipes have been omitted that were similar to others used, and some processes that were rather antiquated have been replaced by more up-to-date ones. Many recipes have been added that are palatable and generally accepted by people in fine health who enjoy fine food. The use of pepper and hot spices has purposely been avoided in the recipes because of their irritating effect on the delicate tissues in the digestive tract.

Many of the recipes in this edition are made with milk

and eggs; however, those of you who are allergic to these foods will find plenty of other dishes which do not use them.

Some of the items in the recipes may be unfamiliar to you. If so, look in the appendix where they have been described and possible sources of supply listed.

We believe this book will be welcomed by an increasingly nutrition-conscious public, ready now to recognize the soybean as tops in nutritional value and an excellent addition to any family's bill of fare.

Dorothea Van Gundy Jones
Arlington, California

THE
VERSATILE
SOYBEAN

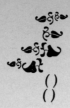

( )
( )

HISTORY OF
THE SOYBEAN

The soybean has a unique history. It can boast of being one of the oldest crops grown by man, and its first mention in Chinese records goes back a little beyond 2000 B.C. Hundreds of books have been written about soybeans, and some 5000 papers have been published concerning various aspects of the soybean industry.

In this brief chapter we can mention only a few interesting highlights in the story of this agricultural crop, which originated in eastern Asia. The soybean is closely associated with the history of China, where it has been almost the sole source of protein for generations. In fact, some historians attribute the existence and survival of China as a nation to her use of the soybean as a food.

The soybean in the United States dates back to 1804, when it was first introduced here; it had been introduced in Europe almost a hundred years earlier. Production in the United States did not reach any sizable figure until 1924, when 5 million bushels were produced. The increase in production since that year has been phenomenal; by 1940 it had reached 78 million bushels. During the war years production doubled, and many predicted that the soybean market had reached its peak and would gradually decline after the war. How wrong these prophets were, for with modern research finding new uses and improved methods, the increase has been steadily upward until today more than 700 million bushels are produced each year.

Although production of soybeans has grown out of proportion to all expectations, demand has also grown in practically the same proportion, and as a result soybeans have never been classed as a surplus crop, as have wheat, cotton, and other major crops.

The United States Department of Agriculture has done much in the development of the soybean industry. Dr. W. J. Morse was one of the early investigators commissioned by the government to go to Asia for research work on the soybean. His work was so extensive and thoroughly carried out as to earn for him the title of "father of the soybean" in the United States. His findings were published in his book *The Soybean*.

Dr. J. A. Leclerc was another research worker connected with the United States Department of Agriculture who contributed a great deal of time and energy to the promotion of this growing industry.

In 1920 the American Soybean Association was organized, primarily as a growers' organization, and it has since become a coordinating agency for the many branches of research within the soybean industry. Each year since its founding the Association has held a national convention somewhere close to the center of production, bringing together speakers from all areas of the industry. The Association has done much through its meetings as well as its monthly publication, *The Soybean Digest*, to stimulate a healthy interest in research, technical know-how, modern and practical methods of production, and general uses of the soybean.

Henry Ford very early saw the possibility of the use of soybean plastics in his fast-growing automobile industry, and since his day the soybean has played no small part in the manufacture of commercial products. Ford also established a research laboratory under the direction of capable chemists to work on various edible products made from the soybean. He made great contributions in this area.

The father of one of the authors, T. A. Van Gundy, became interested in the nutritional value of soybeans while attending the World's Fair in San Francisco in 1915, where they were featured in the Oriental exhibits. Upon going home he purchased some soybeans and began experimenting with them. As far as we know he was the first person on the Pacific Coast to develop a line of commercial foods from this wonder bean. By 1927 he had developed a number of palatable products which he manufactured and sold through health food stores. Soybean foods were virtually unknown at this time, and it took courage and perseverance to put them across.

H. W. Miller, M.D., a missionary doctor in China, was also closely connected with the early history of the soybean. He recognized it as a valuable addition to human nutrition. Almost immediately after his arrival in China in 1902, he became aware of the use of the soybean in the people's diet. The value of his contribution to the use of soy milk, particularly in association with infant feeding, cannot be measured. Dr. Miller worked closely with the

THE VERSATILE SOYBEAN

Soybean
├─ Plants
│ ├─ Green manure
│ ├─ Forage
│ │ ├─ Hay
│ │ ├─ Silage
│ │ └─ Soiling
│ └─ Pasture
│
└─ Beans
   ├─ Meal
   │ ├─ Celluloid substitute
   │ ├─ Stock feed
   │ ├─ Fertilizer
   │ ├─ Human food
   │ │ ├─ Breakfast foods
   │ │ ├─ Diabetic foods
   │ │ ├─ Soy flour ─ Breads, Cakes, Pastry
   │ │ ├─ Infant foods
   │ │ ├─ Macaroni
   │ │ ├─ Crackers
   │ │ ├─ Soy milk
   │ │ ├─ Bean curd
   │ │ ├─ Soy sauce
   │ │ └─ Bean powder
   │ ├─ Glue
   │ ├─ Soy casein
   │ └─ Water paint
   │
   ├─ Oil
   │ ├─ Glycerin
   │ ├─ Enamels
   │ ├─ Food products
   │ │ ├─ Butter substitute
   │ │ ├─ Lard substitute
   │ │ ├─ Edible oils
   │ │ └─ Salad oils
   │ ├─ Varnish
   │ ├─ Waterproof goods
   │ ├─ Linoleum
   │ ├─ Paints
   │ ├─ Soap stock ─ Hard soaps, Soft soaps
   │ ├─ Celluloid
   │ ├─ Rubber substitute
   │ ├─ Printing ink
   │ ├─ Lighting
   │ ├─ Lubricating
   │ ├─ Core binder
   │ ├─ Candles
   │ └─ Lecithin
   │
   ├─ Green beans
   │ ├─ Green vegetable
   │ ├─ Canned vegetable
   │ └─ Salads
   │
   └─ Dried beans
      ├─ Stock feed
      │ ├─ Sheep
      │ ├─ Hogs
      │ ├─ Cattle
      │ └─ Poultry
      ├─ Soy sauce
      ├─ Boiled beans
      ├─ Baked beans
      ├─ Soups
      ├─ Coffee substitute
      ├─ Soy milk
      ├─ Breakfast foods
      ├─ Bean curd
      │ ├─ Fresh
      │ ├─ Dried
      │ ├─ Smoked
      │ └─ Fermented
      ├─ Condensed soy milk
      ├─ Fresh soy milk
      ├─ Confections
      ├─ Soy casein
      │ ├─ Paper sizing
      │ ├─ Paints
      │ ├─ Textile dressing
      │ └─ Waterproofing for textiles
      └─ Soy-milk powder

SOURCE: U.S. Department of Agriculture, Farmers' Bulletin, no. 1617.

Soybean Association and with international agencies in developing and promoting palatable soybean foods for consumption in the United States and in the underdeveloped countries of the world, where protein foods are scarce and hard to come by.

During the war years Dr. Clive M. McCay, professor of nutrition at Cornell University, and his wife did much research and experimental work to find palatable ways of incorporating soybeans into the American diet. They made a real contribution in popularizing this little-known and highly valuable protein food.

In September, 1961, a Conference on Soybean Products for Protein in Human Foods was held at Peoria, Illinois. It was co-sponsored by the U.S. Department of Agriculture Foreign Agriculture Service, the United Nations Children's Fund, and the Soybean Council of America, Inc. (representing the National Soybean Processors' Association and the American Soybean Association). These meetings made a real contribution to the food products area of the industry. The proceedings are reported in a 234-page book published by the U.S. Department of Agriculture Research Service.

Thanks to the work of the able men mentioned in this chapter and many others connected with the industry, the popularity of soybean products has grown by leaps and bounds, until today soybeans are making their contribution to processed and manufactured foods in general. It is the authors' belief that we are just beginning to explore the vast possibilities of the soybean, and that its popularity will continue to grow not only in commercial products but also in the home. It is our hope that this volume will show how the soybean can add to the nutritional value of family menus in the form of exciting but inexpensive new dishes.

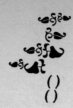

()
()

NUTRITIONAL VALUE

Soybeans can rightfully claim the honor of being one of the most concentrated and nutritious foods known to man. They can make a poor diet good and a good diet better, and they can add zest and variety to vegetarian menus.

Protein Content

Soybeans rank as one of the five great protein foods. The beans are unique in nutritional value because of their high percentage of protein and oil. Not only is the protein high in quantity but it is of good quality, being practically the same in food value as animal protein (meat, milk, fish, and eggs). Chemical analysis shows that soybeans contain in nearly maximum proportions the amino acids essential in the diet of men and animals. This means that soybeans are sufficiently complete to sustain life for an extended period of time. They are the best source of protein from the vegetable kingdom, and can honestly claim the title of "the meat that grows on vines."

The soybean, however, should not be considered primarily as a meat substitute but rather as a protein food that can fortify other foods. It is one of the most economical ways of adding more protein to the diet. This is especially true of soy flour.

Soybeans not only contain high-quality protein, but their protein content is much higher than that of other foods. Compared with other protein foods, soybeans contain

1½ times as much protein as cheese, peas, or navy beans
2 times as much protein as meat, fish, or lima beans
3 times as much protein as eggs or whole wheat flour
11 times as much protein as milk*

Two pounds of low-fat soy flour are equal in protein content to

5 lbs. of boneless meat.
6 doz. eggs.
15 qts. of milk.
4 lbs. of cheese.

Carbohydrate Content

The carbohydrate (starch and sugar) content of the soybean is low, being only one-half that of other dry beans. Much of this carbohydrate is of a kind not well utilized by the body; dry soybeans therefore contain only about 12 percent of available carbohydrate, and the green beans

* Agricultural Development Department of the Baltimore & Ohio Railroad.

count as a 6 percent carbohydrate vegetable. Soybeans contain little starch, and for this reason have always been a logical item in diabetic and starch-restricted diets. In fact, it was the special dietary value of soybeans that first gave them a toehold as a human food in this country. Arriving via the "diet special" proved to be more of a hindrance than a help at first. The public, unaware of their nutritional value, tended in the early years to avoid soybeans until prescribed. Now they are finding their rightful place in the family diet.

Minerals and Vitamins

Soybeans are a protective food in that they contain both vitamins and minerals. They are especially rich in calcium, phosphorus, and iron, and this applies not only to the bean but to soy flour and grits as well. The green beans contain vitamin A, the B vitamins, and some vitamin C. The dry beans have no vitamin C and considerably less vitamin A but almost three times as much of the B vitamins as the green beans. The oil has vitamins A and D and is a good source of vitamins E, F, and K. Vitamin F is really a group of special fat constituents known as unsaturated fatty acids. Soybean oil is one of the more concentrated sources of these fatty acids.

Fat

The dry soybean contains from 18 to 22 percent of fat or oil. It has

  ½ time as much oil as cheese, almonds, or peanuts
   1 time as much oil as average meat

2 times as much oil as eggs
5 times as much oil as milk
10 times as much oil as whole wheat flour

Lecithin

Another virtue of the soybean is that it contains lecithin, a fat-soluble substance containing phosphorus and choline, both essential for normal body functions. The lecithin content of the soybean has made it valuable in certain corrective diets. Lecithin itself is not a new discovery. It was originally extracted from egg yolks, but for the past 20 years the commercial source has been soybeans. It is used in making bread, shortening, candy, and ice cream to promote smooth blending and prevent rancidity. It acts as an emulsifier, breaking up fat particles and oil globules and spreading them evenly throughout a food product.

No one is exactly sure how lecithin works in the human body. Research in such centers as New York University, Northwestern University, and the University of Chicago has indicated that among other things it helps disperse deposits of fatty materials and cholesterol in certain vital organs. It is believed by some to play an important role in the absorption, transport in the bloodstream, and utilization of fats and fatlike substances. It is also known to be an important component of the sheath around brain and nerve cells. It is rich in substances which are important for the proper functioning of all living cells in the body.

Many doctors have suggested the use of lecithin in the treatment of skin and nerve disorders and of hardening of the arteries and in general body-building diets. At first it came in liquid form, resembling a heavy dark oil or grease. Often this was encased in a gelatin capsule. It is now in pleasant, easy-to-take granular form, which may be stirred into any liquid as milk or juice.

Alkaline Ash

Last but not least on the nutritional side is the fact that soybeans are alkaline in their ash, being rich in potassium and other alkaline-bearing salts. This has made them valuable in many corrective diets.

Economy

Soybeans are an excellent means of making a low-cost diet nutritionally safe. They are one of our cheapest sources of nutritious protein. A few cents' worth of dry beans will serve four to six persons and give them the food value of greater quantities of meat or fish. Soy flour or grits, at the cost of a few cents, can step up the protein content of a dish to equal the more expensive animal protein foods.

Abbreviations Used in This Book

doz. dozen
g. grams
lb(s). pound(s)

oz. ounce(s)
pkg(s). package(s)
pt(s). pint(s)

qt(s). quart(s)
tbs. tablespoon(s)
tsp. teaspoon(s)

Oven Temperatures (in Fahrenheit)

Slow or cool oven	250 to 350 degrees
Moderate or medium oven	350 to 400 degrees
Hot oven	400 to 450 degrees
Very hot oven	450 to 500 degrees

Cooking Terms

Boil—to cook at a rolling boil, over moderate flame.

Broil—to cook under flame in broiler part of oven.

Chill—to refrigerate food until cold, but not frozen.

Liquefy—to use commercial liquefier or blender.

Pressure cook—to prepare food in commercial pressure cooker, following manufacturer's instructions which come with the implement.

Purée—to boil until soft and rub through sieve.

Roast—to cook food in oven rather than on top of stove.

Sauté—to fry lightly, turning frequently, until tender but not brown.

Simmer—to cook over low heat at just below boil.

Steam—to cook over steam; food often placed in sieve or muslin bag over boiling water.

Toast—to brown in pan without shortening, either over hot heat or in slow oven.

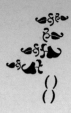

SOUP
TO NUTS

Soybeans may be used green, dry, whole, cracked, powdered, or sprouted, and as meat, milk, cheese, bread, or oil, with coffee, candy, and nuts thrown in for good measure. The old phrase "from soup to nuts" is very fitting and descriptive of this Oriental bean.

Green Soybeans

When the beans have nearly reached full size but are still green and succulent, they are a most palatable, nutritious, low-starch green vegetable. They have a nutlike flavor, and may be used by themselves or mixed with other vegetables. Green soybeans are canned or frozen and may be purchased in all stores or markets carrying soy products. The average green soybean contains

Water	70.00%
Protein	12.25%

Fat	5.22%
Total carbohydrate (by difference)	11.07%
Fiber	1.30%
Sugars	4.18%
Ash	1.52%
Calories per pound	636 *

Dry Soybeans

Dry soybeans are the mature beans removed from the pods. The edible types vary in size and color. They are a medium-sized round bean, usually yellow, greenish-yellow, or gray-green in color.

Because of their high protein content, dry soybeans require long cooking. The dry beans may be cooked at home and are delicious when thoroughly done and properly seasoned. Dry soybeans are canned by several firms, and those seasoned with tomatoes are very popular. The cooking time varies with the variety of the bean, but it will be several hours in the ordinary pan. Many quick-cook varieties have been developed in the last few years. Cook them according to the directions on the package. It is always wise to soak the beans first. Some cooks prefer to soak the beans for 24 hours and keep them in the refrigerator to prevent fermentation. The easiest and quickest way is the pressure cooker; the average soaked bean will be soft in 45 minutes of pressure cooking.

The secret of any soybean dish is the proper seasoning, for the beans themselves are rather flat in taste and need added flavor in the form of yeast extract seasoning, soy sauce, onions, celery, or tomatoes.

* Agricultural Experiment Station, University of Illinois.

Soybeans vary in protein, fat, and carbohydrate content, but the average dry or mature bean contains approximately

Water	8–14%
Protein	33–42%
Fat	18–22%
Carbohydrate, including fiber	25–32%
Ash	3.5–6%
Calories per pound	1590–1993 *

Because much of the carbohydrate is not well utilized by the body, it is estimated that only about 12 percent is available carbohydrate.

Roasted Soybeans

Roasted beans resemble salted peanuts, and are known as salted, toasted, or roasted soybeans. They are usually deep-fat fried and then salted. They will stay fresh and crisp for a long time if kept in an airtight container. They may be used as any salted nut. When ground they are a good addition to cookies, cakes, and other desserts.

Sprouted Soybeans

Sprouted soybeans became headline news in World War II. Dr. Clive M. McCay, of the School of Nutrition at Cornell University, stressed soybean and soy sprouts as

* U.S. Department of Agriculture, *Composition of Foods*, Handbook 8.

one answer to the meat shortage problem. Dr. McCay worked with Dr. Peng Chen Hsu, a Chinese student at Cornell. Their findings were presented at a soybean luncheon given by Governor and Mrs. Thomas Dewey in the executive mansion at Albany, New York. The great value of the sprouts is that they are a delicious protein food, an excellent source of vitamin C, which serves as a fresh vegetable in the diet. The sprouted bean contains all the vitamin B complex of the original bean plus the vitamin C that forms in all sprouted foods. There is some evidence that sprouting increases the riboflavin and niacin contents and that vitamin A is liberated.

Bean sprouts are not an unusual vegetable in markets on the West Coast or in areas where there is an Oriental population. They may also be sprouted at home (see recipes). A trip through a bean sprout factory is both fascinating and enlightening. The beans triple in weight and quadruple in bulk, literally pushing themselves out of the containers used for sprouting.

The Cow of China—Soy Milk

Soy milk is one of the most unusual and interesting of the many different versions of the soybean. This milk has been made in China for generations. The dry beans are soaked and ground; water is added, and then strained off after cooking. Equipment for this process has been and in many places still is primitive and crude. The milk has a rather strong bean flavor; however, the Orientals have acquired a taste for it and have used soy milk as a staple food for generations. The value of this food has long been recognized, and today in both the United States and

China its bean taste and odor have been removed so that soy milk now is sweet, pleasant, and rather nutlike in flavor, not greatly different from pasteurized dairy milk. Various food elements can be added as needed to make it equal to cow's milk. Baby formulas equivalent to mother's milk are made of it.

Soy milk and its development can hardly be mentioned without thinking of Harry W. Miller, M.D., a Seventh-Day Adventist missionary doctor who spent more than half a century in China. He early became interested in nutrition as a means of helping the Chinese to a better life. Looking around for local plant foods, he began working with the soybean and especially the milk. He developed processes to make the milk more palatable. Clinical work in China showed soybean milk to be an excellent food for babies where dairy milk was not available. Dr. Miller's own story, *China Doctor*, published by Harper & Bros., tells in detail his fascinating experiences.

Certainly Dr. Miller has done more than any other person to introduce soybeans and soybean products, especially the milk, to the population of this country. As director of research for the International Nutrition Research Foundation of Arlington, California, he has been working closely with various food companies in the development of palatable and nutritious soy foods.

Soy milk has been recommended by physicians for years to patients who are allergic to cow's milk, and now it is being recommended to those who have suffered or are high risks for degenerative heart disease and who need a milk with unsaturated fat as a replacement for dairy milk. Soy milk certainly is the answer for these cases. Let us state here, however, that soy milk is so palatable and of such high nutritional value that it may be highly recommended to anyone seeking a delicious new beverage and a good food.

✑ KINDS OF SOY MILK

Soy milk may be made at home by several different methods described later on in the book.

Commercially there two different methods for making soy milk. The most nutritional one follows somewhat the same general method used for generations in the Orient—dry beans are soaked, ground, and boiled, and the water extraction is taken off. This makes a liquid containing practically all the nutritional value of the soybean except the fiber.

The other method is to compound the formula from an isolated protein extracted from soybeans. Carbohydrates, fats, vitamins, and minerals are then added to bring up the nutritional value. From a nutritionist's standpoint, the water extraction method seems to be the better of the two.

Some commercial soy powders are sold for making milk at home by just the addition of water; however, these do not make palatable soy milk, and unless properly cooked they are not very digestible. Soybeans and soy products must be thoroughly cooked in order to be of the most value nutritionally.

Soy milk is sold commercially in single-strength liquid and liquid concentrate (which can be used as cream or diluted with equal amounts of water), or it may be purchased in powder form (all-purpose or malt flavor).

There are many baby formulas on the market made

from soy milk, and there is a high-protein formula low in sugar, salt, and fat for those requiring a special formula of this type.

"The Meat Without a Bone"—Tofu or Soy Cheese

Tofu or soy cheese is more commonly known in the Orient as bean curd. It is a soft, custardy white cheese made from soy milk that is definitely exotic in flavor. A common food in the diet of the Chinese and Japanese, fresh tofu can always be had in sections of the country with a high Oriental population. The Chinese have aptly described it as "the meat without a bone."

Soy curd is the coagulated plant casein of the soybean, made from soy milk, very much as we make cottage cheese. It is a soft, easily digested food, fairly high in protein, and can be used as cheese, as a meat or fish substitute, or even as a dessert. When fresh, it is a tasteless product, decidedly flat and watery, but when properly prepared and seasoned, it is delicious as well as different and inexpensive.

Fresh tofu contains approximately

Water	80%
Protein	10%
Carbohydrate	5%
Fat	4%
Minerals	1%

One cake of soybean curd (2¾″ × 2½″ by 1″, 120 g.) contains 8.4 grams of protein.

Tofu or soy curd is also canned commercially. Soy sauce, yeast extract seasonings, or pimientos are added for flavor, and each brand varies in texture, taste, and ingredients. It may be used as a sandwich spread or in salads, or it may be added to salad dressings. It is also used in many entree recipes, including the famous Japanese dish suki-yaki. When scrambled, tofu makes a good replacement, for scrambled eggs.

The Little Giant Among Protein Foods— Soy Flour

The best-known and the most valuable product of the versatile soybean is soy flour. In spite of the fact that the soybean has been the nutritional backbone of the Orient, the flour is largely an Occidental product. The Chinese have used their stone mills for wheat, corn, and other grains, but not for the soybean. Soy flour had its beginning in Vienna under the guidance of Dr. Laszlo Berczeller, who saw its possibilities as a cheap nutritious food for the starving people of Europe.

Germany perhaps has done more with soy flour than any other nation in Europe, and it is in the further development of soy flour that we have added the American touch to the ancient bean. The flour is the soy product that will prove the most valuable to us—a food of the future. This product, an achievement of nature and science, can mean better nutrition for the entire world.

Soy flour is not a true flour in the sense that wheat and rye flours are. It is better described as a highly concentrated vegetable protein food derived from soybeans, and it is more nearly comparable in concentration of food value and in use to dry powdered milk or dry powdered eggs. One glance at the list below, drawn up by the Soy Flour Association, reveals its right to reign as king of the proteins. The normal daily protein requirement is 65 to 100 grams.

	Grams of Protein per Pound of Food
Low-fat soy flour (or grits)	225
Full-fat soy flour (or bean meats)	182
Peanut butter	118
American cheese	109
Navy beans	100
Lean beefsteak	90
Halibut	86
Lean pork chops	82
Salmon	80
Frankfurters	68
Eggs	59
Pork sausage	54
Pecan meats	43

Compared with patent wheat flour, soy flour is 15 times as rich in calcium, 7 times as rich in phosphorus, 10 times as rich in iron, 10 times as rich in thiamine, 9 times as rich in riboflavin, and 5 times as rich in niacin, besides being 4 to 5 times as rich in total minerals.

Americans are just beginning to appreciate the value of soy flour and what it can mean in the human diet. This flour is the richest in protein of all known foods except dried egg whites, and it is one of the richest sources per pound of the entire vitamin B complex. It has a very high content of calcium, phosphorus, and potassium, as well as liberal supplies of copper, magnesium, and available iron. The full-fat flour also contains lecithin. Soy flour is almost starch-free and gives an appreciable alkaline reaction. In addition to all this, it is the lowest in cost of any of the common protein foods.

There are two general types of soy flour: full-fat and low-fat flour. The full-fat contains all the natural fat of the soybean, that is, approximately 20 percent. This flour has a high calorie content because of the fat, and contains 40 to 45 percent of protein. The low-fat flour is the same product but with much or practically all of the fat removed. Some flours contain as little as 1 percent of fat, while in others 5 to 7 percent of the fat remains. The concentration of protein is higher in the low-fat flour, ranging from 47 to 54 percent, and is of a high order of digestibility. Full-fat and low-fat flours are largely interchangeable in recipes.

The uses of soy flour are many, and it appears in many unexpected places and products. The candy industry uses it in fudge, caramels, kisses, and crunch-type candies in percentages of from 3 to 10 to aid in better emulsification of the fats in the candy and to prevent the finished product from drying out. Soy flour is a natural product for dietary foods; it has been used by this industry for many years because of its low starch content and alkaline ash. It is also used in many infant foods and special foods for the soft diet. The brewing industry has been trying it out as a foam stabilizer in the manufacture of beer. The baking industry has discovered it to be an excellent addition to sweet goods, cakes, pie crusts, and doughnuts, as well as to breads and rolls. It has found its way into macaroni, noodles, and spaghetti and many ready-prepared soups.

Muffin, biscuit, pancake, and waffle mixes with soy are

now on the market and are proving very popular. The meat industry has made substantial use of soy flour in meat loaves and meat preparations. Concentrated foods and army rations have opened up an entirely new field, and these uses can be applied in mass feeding if necessary. Soy bread is the best-known and most common of all soy products, and it is made by many bakeries, although it is still consumed in comparatively small quantities.

Soy flour is creamy yellow in color and rather nutty in taste, and it is fascinating to work with. Like wheat flour, it should be sifted before measuring. It is fluffy and lighter than wheat flour, one cupful weighing about 75 grams as compared with 100 grams for soft wheat flour or 113 grams for hard wheat flour. Soy flour takes up more moisture than wheat flour, and as a result has the advantage of giving a moist product that keeps fresh a long time. A little more salt should be used with soy flour. It cannot be used alone for bread because it has no gluten or starch to bind the mixture together, nor will it replace wheat flour in thickening sauces and gravies. Foods containing soy brown easily and should be baked at a slightly lower temperature.

The Soy Flour Association suggests that soy flour be added in small amounts as one would add eggs or milk. Two tablespoons of the flour in each cup of wheat flour makes a mix that can be used in practically every recipe. Excellent results can be obtained, however, by using much more soy flour—20, 30, even 50 percent may be used in some recipes. Muffins and pancakes can be made from all soy flour if desired. Although the result is not so light and tasty as when only part soy is used, these recipes are valuable for certain special diets. Frequently 100 percent soy flour products, usually containing eggs and milk, are suggested in place of meat and fish in the diet.

Soy Grits and Bits

Grits are the ground or cracked beans and should not be confused with quick-cooking grits or soy bits, as they are often called. The first is the cracked bean, and requires long cooking. The other resembles low-fat soy flour in taste and food value, and cooks in 3 to 5 minutes. Grits can be used as a cereal or to fortify grain cereals with extra protein. They are fine for soups, stews, and meat replacement dishes, and to fortify other foods. They are excellent meat enrichers and stretchers, and for this reason have been used in the meat industry for many years and were used in Lend-Lease sausages and other foods.

Soy grits with their high protein content make excellent meat replacement dishes by themselves and can be made into loaves, patties, vegetable sausages, and "hamburgers" at a cost far below that of the cheapest cuts of meat. When used this way, they need a meatlike seasoning as a finishing touch; the addition of onion or tomatoes is also appetizing.

The grits are also a good addition to vegetable and other soups. Added a little before the soup is done, they enrich any soup with protein at a moment's notice. Soy grits are also excellent in casserole dishes baked with vegetables, and they can be made into a good hash. The grits can even take the place of cheese, as to food value, in a casserole dish; they will add one and a half times as much protein as an equal amount of cheese.

✌ৡ PUFFED GRITS

Certain types of soy grits can be puffed or exploded by a process similar to that used for puffing wheat and rice. The result is a grit larger and lighter in weight that can be used in many ways. Some of these grits are toasted and sold as a ready-to-eat low-starch cereal. They are a valuable addition to cereals as they increase the protein content. They are also fine on a starch-restricted diet. The best selection of grits will be found in specialty food stores.

Soy Oil and Soy Butter

Soybean oil has become one of the important oils of this country, both for food and in industry. Great quantities are used in margarine and shortening, and it has also become one of the popular salad oils. At first it was sold only in dietary food stores, but today it is sold under various trade names in all markets. Soy oil is light golden in color, a good substitute for olive oil. It is excellent as a salad oil and for baking and cooking.

Soy butter is made from finely ground beans or toasted soy flour and soy oil. The oil is beaten into the flour and the result is a light gold butter that can be used in the same way as peanut butter. Some prefer to sweeten it with a small amount of honey. Soy butter has the food value of the soy flour plus the added oil.

Meat Replacement Foods

There are any number of canned vegetable protein foods on the market containing soybeans in some form. Most often the beans or bean products are mixed with other vegetable proteins as gluten and nuts. They are prepared so as to have the protein content of meat and are seasoned to taste as much like meat as possible. They come in all forms, from a loaf to be sliced to a soy wiener.

Sandwich Spreads

There are several ready-prepared sandwich spreads made from soy cheese, soy grits, and ground soybeans. They may be mildly seasoned or spiced and smoked to resemble bologna. They are delicious, of especial value to those who do not use animal products. They add variety to the diet at little cost.

Malts

Soy malts, plain or flavored, have been popular sellers. They are added to milk for a relaxing nightcap or nourishing drink. The base is usually the finely ground low-fat soy flour or powder flavored with vanilla, chocolate, almonds, coconut, carol, or banana. Some are also fortified with extra minerals and other food elements.

Coffee Substitutes

Heavily roasted and ground soybeans are not new as a coffee substitute for those who seek coffeelike beverages free from caffeine. Every dietary food store stocks several coffee substitutes made from soybeans. Heavily roasted and ground soybeans look exactly like coffee but of course are different in aroma and flavor. These roasted beans may be used as a beverage by themselves or mixed with dried fruits, grains, chicory, and other products. Some of the 100 percent soy beverages are in powder form and dissolve instantly in hot water; others are ground for drip, percolating, or silex coffee makers.

Soy Sauce

This ancient seasoning is perhaps the best known of all the soy products because it graces the table of almost every restaurant serving Eastern cuisine in the nation. Soy sauce is made from the whole beans, and its dark color and flavor are the result of the manufacturing process and aging.

Soy sauce may be used for seasoning vegetables, soups, gravies and sauces, sandwich spreads, and salad dressings as well as rice and other carbohydrate foods. It is salty to the taste, and allowance for the salt content must be made when it is used in cooking.

Other Soy Products

Soybean products are constantly being improved, and new uses and foods are coming on the market continuously. Soy albumen, one of the newer products, is made to replace egg albumen in candy manufacture. The Glidden Co. now has a product that contains on a dry basis 96.6 percent protein. Such products have many uses, and we will meet them in special supplement foods as well as in soups, cereals, desserts, and the like where extra protein can be added.

The soybean had a hard time securing a place in the American diet, but there is no question now of its being here to stay. We may not eat many of the beans in their original form, but since they can invade practically everything potable and edible—from coffee to candy—we never know just where we are going to meet them next. Nutritionally these soy additions are an excellent plus factor in our diet.

SOYBEAN RECIPES

()
()

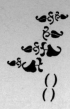

GREEN
SOYBEANS

Green soybeans are a most palatable and nutritious vegetable with a pleasant firm texture and nutty flavor. Their 6 percent available carbohydrate places them in the low-starch class of vegetables. Green soybeans can be cooked and used like green lima beans or peas, and their protein content makes them a welcome addition to less nutritious foods.

Boiled Green Soybeans Remove the beans from their pods. To make hulling easier, pour boiling water over the pods and let them stand 3 to 5 minutes. Drain the pods, break them crosswise, and squeeze out the beans. Cook them as you would green peas or lima beans. Add a small amount of boiling water to the beans; then salt, cover, and boil them until tender. Time varies with the variety of the bean. Some cook in 15 minutes; others take 30 minutes or more. Avoid overcooking. Cooked green soybeans will have a firm texture and will not become mushy, as peas or lima beans do, even after long cooking. Season and serve.

Steamed Green Soybeans   Steam the beans until tender, using no water; add desired seasoning.

Green Beans Cooked in Pods   Green soybeans are sometimes cooked and served in the pods. They are eaten with the fingers. The pods need thorough washing to free them from grit that may cling to the fuzzy surface. After washing, drop the pods into boiling salt water. Cover and boil until the beans are tender; if desired, slip them out by pressing the pods between thumb and finger. Season to taste.

Canned or Frozen Green Soybeans   Canned green soybeans are sold in many large markets and in all specialty food shops. They may be served as a low-starch vegetable and are delicious hot or cold. Serve them as plain beans, or use them in soups, salads, and meat replacement dishes.

In some markets frozen green soybeans can be purchased. These should be cooked according to the directions on the package.

Green Soybean Recipes

⋙ SOYBEAN SOUP

Cooked green soybeans may be added to any soup, or they may be made into soup by themselves by mashing or liquefying with water, milk (dairy or soy), or tomato juice. Add your favorite seasoning. Here is a delicious recipe:

3 tbs. minced onion
1 tsp. oil
1 cup raw or cooked grated carrots
Chopped parsley
4 cups tomato juice
2 cups cooked green soybeans
Pinch sweet basil
Salt to taste

Sauté onion in oil, add carrot, and continue cooking over a low flame for a few minutes. Add tomato juice, mashed or whole soybeans, and seasonings. Simmer 8 to 10 minutes. Serve hot with garnish of parsley. Serves 4.

◦§ FRESH SUCCOTASH

2 cups shelled green soybeans
2 cups fresh or frozen corn kernels
1 cup cold water
½ cup cream
Salt and other seasoning as desired

Place beans in pan and add cold water. Boil until beans are almost done. Then add corn kernels that have been cut from cob with a sharp knife; add cream. Cook 5 to 10 minutes. Season with salt and other seasonings to taste, and serve hot. Serves 4 or 5.

Green peppers and/or pimiento may also be added to vary this dish. Canned green soybeans may be used in place of fresh beans.

⋅εઉ SCALLOPED GREEN SOYBEANS

Cooked green soybeans
White sauce
Melba toast crumbs

Fill baking dish with cooked green soybeans. Add white sauce to almost cover. Top with crumbs and bake in moderate oven 20 minutes.

As variations, use equal parts of cooked soybeans and cooked carrots, or equal parts of cooked soybeans and cooked celery.

⋅εઉ GREEN SOY FRITTERS

2 cups cooked green soybeans
2 tsp. powdered vegetable broth
2 eggs
Salt as desired

Mash green beans well and add to beaten eggs. Add powdered vegetable broth and season with a small amount of salt. Bake as fritters on a hot, heavy, slightly oiled grill. Allow to brown on one side and then turn. Serve hot with tomato sauce or brown gravy. Serves 4 to 6.

⋅εઉ GREEN SOYBEAN CASSEROLE

Put cooked green soybeans in baking dish. Cover with half-circles of vegetable bologna or nut loaf. Top each slice with a half-round of sliced pineapple. Bake in moderate oven until heated through—20 to 30 minutes.

◄§ GREEN SOYBEANS WITH ONIONS

2 cups cooked green soybeans
2 tbs. chopped onion
2 tbs. oil

Brown onion in oil. Add cooked green soybeans, and heat mixture thoroughly. Serve hot as a vegetable. Serves 4.

◄§ MEXICAN BURGERS

2 cups cooked green soybeans
1 can (6-oz.) tomato paste
1 cup tomato juice
2 cups vegetable burger
½ cup chopped onions
Garlic, oregano, cumin, M.S.G.*

Mix all ingredients, using seasonings to taste. Cook slowly for 15 minutes, stirring often to blend flavors. Serve hot over toasted burger buns. Serves 6.

◄§ GREEN SOYBEAN SALAD

2 cups cooked green soybeans, drained
1 pimiento, chopped fine
1 tbs. chopped parsley
Mayonnaise to moisten
½ cup chopped celery
1 tbs. green or dry onion, cut fine

Mix together, chill, and serve with salad greens. As a variation, add raw shredded carrots. Serves 4 to 6.

* Monosodium glutamate. See Appendix.

✒ﾟ MOLDED GREEN SOYBEAN SALAD

   1 pkg. lemon- or lime-flavored vegetable gelatin
   1 cup cooked green soybeans (canned or fresh), drained
   1 cup chopped celery
   1 cup finely shredded raw carrots

Make vegetable gelatin according to directions on package. When partly thickened, add mixed vegetables. Green peppers may also be added. Pour mixture into large shallow pan or individual molds. Chill until firm. Serve on lettuce with desired dressing. Serves 4.

✒ﾟ GREEN SOYBEAN AND CUCUMBER SALAD

   2 cups cooked green soybeans, drained
   2 cups diced cucumber
   1 cup shredded carrots
   Mayonnaise or desired dressing
   Leaf lettuce
   Sliced tomatoes

Mix soybeans, cucumber, and carrots. Add dressing. Mix well and serve from lettuce-lined bowl on platter. Decorate with sliced tomatoes. Serves 4 to 6.

✒ﾟ COMBINATION SALAD BOWL

   2 cups cooked green soybeans (canned or fresh), drained
   1 cup chopped celery
   1 cup shredded raw carrots
   Asparagus tips
   Romaine lettuce
   Watercress
   Tomatoes

Mix soybeans, celery, carrots, and desired amount of shredded romaine lettuce, watercress, and sliced tomatoes. Moisten with French or mayonnaise dressing. Fill shallow salad bowl, top with asparagus tips, sprigs of watercress, and tomato wedges. Serves 4 to 6.

❧ ADDITIONAL USES OF GREEN SOYBEANS

Add a cup of cooked green soybeans to your favorite tossed salad.

Liquefy green soybeans and use in soup.

Mash green soybeans and use over toast.

Use green soybeans in your favorite chili recipe instead of regular beans.

Bake green soybeans with your favorite tomato sauce.

❧ SOYBEAN VEGETABLE SALAD

Cooked green soybeans may be mixed with any raw or cooked vegetable, such as carrots, celery, cauliflower, beets, peas, cabbage, cucumber, and tomatoes. Season with favorite dressing. Decorate with ripe olives, radish roses, and watercress.

❧ GREEN SOYBEAN SANDWICH FILLING

2 cups cooked mashed green soybeans
1 tbs. chopped celery
2 tbs. mayonnaise
1 tbs. chopped green onions

Mix ingredients thoroughly and use as spread on toast or crackers or in sandwiches.

☙ SOYBEAN AND TAHINI DIP

2 cups cooked green soybeans
Juice of 1 lemon
1 tbs. chopped parsley
Sprinkle of garlic
3 tbs. tahini (sesame butter)
Mixed herbs
Salt to taste

Liquefy green soybeans; add tahini, lemon juice, parsley, and salt. Mix thoroughly. Use as a dip for celery or any raw vegetable or as a spread for toast or crackers. May be used in place of butter or margarine.

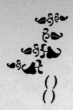

DRY
SOYBEANS

Dry soybeans require long cooking. Always soak them overnight. Soybeans require some kind of extra seasoning in the form of soy sauce, yeast extract seasonings, pimiento, or tomatoes. Soaked, a cup of dry beans will make 2½ to 3 cups. One teaspoonful of salt is about right for each cup of dry beans. Soy sauce and yeast extract flavorings are salty. If they are used, it is wise to cut the amount of salt in half.

Before cooking dry soybeans, look over the beans and remove all foreign particles, and then wash them well. Place them in a bowl and cover them with water. Soak them overnight or for several hours. Adding salt when soaking the soybeans will cut the cooking time.

Try using meat tenderizer in soaking beans or add some to the beans after they are cooked. Let them stand for several hours. This sometimes helps to remove some of the gas-forming properties of beans.

Pressure Cooking Pour beans, with water used for soaking, into a pressure cooker. Add salt and yeast extract seasoning, cover, and cook 30 to 45 minutes at 10-15 lbs. pressure.

Top-of-Stove Cooking Place the soaked and salted beans in a heavy pan. Almost cover with water. Cook for several hours or until beans are tender, adding water as needed; season, and serve hot or cold.

Baking Soybeans Place half-cooked soybeans in a baking dish, and add seasoning and enough liquid to cover them. Cover the pan and bake the beans in a moderate oven for several hours or until they are done. Remove the lid during the last half-hour of baking.

Freezer Method Soak dry soybeans overnight, and then put them in the freezer with the water in which they have been soaked. Freeze overnight, or as long as you desire. Remove them from the freezer and cook them as you choose until they are tender. Freezing cuts the cooking time. Be sure to use a straight-sided container for freezing so the beans will slip out easily for cooking.

Dry Soybean Recipes

◄§ COOKED DRY SOYBEANS

- 1 cup dry soybeans
- 3 or more cups water
- 1 heaping tsp. powdered vegetable broth, or 3 tbs. minced celery
- ½ tsp. salt

1 tsp. yeast extract flavoring, or 1 tbs. soy sauce
1 tbs. whole wheat flour

Wash beans and soak overnight in 3 cups salted cold water. Cook in same water, adding more if necessary. Pour beans and water into pressure cooker, and add seasoning. Cook about 45 minutes. Adjust seasoning. If gravy is desired, add ½ cup more water before cooking. When done, drain off liquid and thicken it with 1 tbs. whole wheat flour. Add beans and reheat. If using ordinary pan, not pressure cooker, cook beans several hours, adding more water as needed. Serves 4.

◆§ SOYBEANS WITH TOMATO SAUCE

4 cups cooked soybeans
1 cup tomato juice

Combine the cooked soybeans, prepared according to the recipe above, with the tomato juice. Simmer until flavors are blended. Tomato sauce or soup may be used instead of juice, and other seasonings may be added to taste.

◆§ CANNED OR BAKED SOYBEANS

Canned or baked soybeans are now available in most markets, either plain or in tomato sauce. They may be served like any baked beans and are good hot or cold. The plain beans are more flavorsome when heated with tomatoes or various sauces.

A Boston baked soybean is now available. This product is delicious and very popular.

✍ SOYBEANS WITH ONIONS AND CELERY

1 cup dry soybeans
3 or more cups water
1 cup chopped celery
1 medium-sized onion, sliced
1 tbs. soy sauce
¾ tsp. salt
1 tsp. powdered vegetable broth
1 tbs. whole wheat flour

Wash beans and soak overnight in 2 cups salted water.
Add 1 cup water, and cook in pressure cooker until three-
quarters done, adding more water if necessary. Then add
chopped celery, sliced onion, soy sauce, and broth. Continue cooking until done. Drain off liquid and thicken
with whole wheat flour. Add beans and heat before serving. For tomato flavor, replace cooking water with 1 cup
tomato juice or pulp. If using ordinary pan, cook beans
until almost done before adding celery and onions. Onions
may be omitted, and more celery used instead. A few
minced ripe olives may be added if desired. Serves 4.

✍ SAVORY SANDWICH FILLING

Press cooked soybeans through a sieve or put through a
food grinder. Stir in enough thin mayonnaise, boiled
salad dressing or milk to make a smooth paste. Mix with
finely chopped onions and seasoning to taste.

As a topping for melba toast or crackers, Savory Sandwich Filling is an excellent appetizer or between-meals
snack. Olives stuffed with pimiento and cut in quarters
may be used as a garnish. Or crumble crisp bacon and
sprinkle on top.

◄§ BAKED SOYBEANS 1

  2 cups dry soybeans
  6 cups water
  2 tsp. salt
  2 tbs. molasses
  1 tbs. powdered vegetable broth, or ¼ cup finely minced
    celery

Wash and soak beans in salted water overnight. Cook until almost done. Drain, and save water. Place beans in casserole or bean pot. Put broth and molasses in measuring cup and fill with water from the beans. Pour mixture over beans, adding more water to almost cover. Cover and bake 2 to 3 hours in moderate oven. Serves 4 to 6. For 2 or 3 persons, cut recipe in half or prepare the whole recipe and freeze half of it for future use.

◄§ BAKED SOYBEANS 2

  2 cups dry soybeans
  6 cups water
  1 tsp. salt
  1 tbs. powdered vegetable broth
  4 tbs. finely minced celery
  2 tbs. soy sauce
  Tomato juice

Wash and soak beans in salted water overnight. Cook until almost done. Drain. Pour beans in casserole or bean pot and mix with powdered vegetable broth and minced celery. Add tomato juice to almost cover and bake covered in a slow oven for several hours. For the last hour, remove the cover. Top with sliced tomatoes 15 minutes before removing from the oven. Serves 4.

◄§ BAKED SOYBEANS AND ONIONS

2 cups dry soybeans
6 cups water
1 large onion, sliced
1 tsp. salt
2 cups tomato juice
2 tbs. oil
1 tbs. soy or meatlike sauce
Tomato sauce

Wash and soak beans in salted water overnight. Cook until done. Slice onion and brown in oil. Add soy or meatlike sauce and tomato juice. Cook a few minutes. Place drained beans in casserole, add tomato sauce, and bake uncovered in slow oven 1 hour or more. Serves 4.

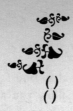

()
()

ROASTED
OR TOASTED
SOYBEANS

Salted toasted soybeans are delicious and can be used like any salted nut. Several brands are for sale in retail stores, but they can readily be prepared at home.

Roasted Soybean Recipes

◦§ SALTED SOYBEANS

Because soybeans contain so much protein and fat, they are good fried in deep fat and salted to serve like salted nuts. Any of the good table varieties may be used. Wash and soak the dry beans overnight, then drain them and spread them out at room temperature until they are dry on the surface. Fry a few at a time in deep fat at 350° for 8 to 10 minutes. Drain on absorbent paper and sprinkle with salt while still warm. Add a sprinkle of M.S.G.

◆⟋ OVEN-ROASTED SOYBEANS

Soak beans overnight in salted water. Boil for 1 hour in same water. Drain. Spread in shallow pan and roast in 350° oven for 30 minutes or until brown. Sprinkle with M.S.G. while warm.

◆⟋ GROUND TOASTED SOYBEANS

Toasted soybeans when ground in a food mill can be used in a variety of recipes. Grind beans using medium-fine knife. If not used at once, store in tightly covered jar.

◆⟋ SOY TOPPING

Use ground toasted soybeans as topping for desserts, puddings, ice creams, or salads.

◆⟋ CEREALS

Add ground toasted soybeans to ready-to-eat cereals, or serve a small amount as a 100 percent soy-nut cereal with cream or milk.

◆⟋ SOY NUTS

Ground toasted soybeans may be used as chopped nuts in candies, frostings, cookies, and so forth.

◆⟋ SOY OMELET

Add 1 tbs. ground toasted soybeans for each egg. Follow your favorite omelet recipe.

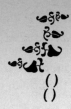

SPROUTED
SOYBEANS

The Second World War brought sprouted soybeans into the limelight. They are the field or garden beans with a 2- or 3-inch sprout, containing all the nutritious food value of the beans plus the vitamin C developed in sprouting. The dry beans may be sprouted as needed. Some authorities regard them as our best edible form of soybeans.

Sprouted soybeans are very tender, and make an excellent meat substitute or a delicious salad vegetable. They may be eaten cooked or raw, and are a good addition to omelets, soufflés, stews, and fricassees. The sprouts require only a few minutes' cooking; to preserve their crispness, they should not be added to hot mixtures until a few minutes before serving.

Soy sprouts are now sold in many markets, but they may easily be sprouted at home. All that is necessary is a covered container with good drainage in which the beans can be flooded with lukewarm water several times a day. Beans placed uncovered in a small amount of water to sprout turn brown and rot before the sprouts are formed. The following directions for sprouting are from the U. S. Department of Agriculture and the School of Nutrition, Cornell University.

Methods of Sprouting Soybeans

Department of Agriculture Method Soybeans (mung bean variety) can be sprouted in a flowerpot, a sink strainer, or any container that has holes in it for drainage. Be sure the container is large enough, for the beans swell to at least six times their original bulk as they sprout. Soak overnight, and next morning put the beans in the container, cover, and leave them in a warm place. Flood with lukewarm water at least four or five times each day during the sprouting period. In 4 to 6 days the sprouts will be 2 to 3 inches long. Then they should be kept in a cool place, just like any fresh vegetable.*

McCay Step-by-Step Process for Sprouting Dr. Clive M. McCay, of the School of Nutrition at Cornell University and the New York State Emergency Food Commission, has done much to popularize soy sprouts. Directions for growing them follow. Secure a bean that will sprout quickly and use a little chlorinated lime to prevent mold. Beans older than one year will not sprout well. Beans are less likely to mold if sufficient air is allowed for proper ventilation.

1. Sort beans, removing broken pieces and other seeds.
2. Wash beans.

* U. S. Department of Agriculture, *Bulletin*, No. 166.

3. Soak beans overnight in lukewarm water to cover. For 1 lb. of beans use 3 pts. water and add a pinch of chlorinated lime. For 20 lbs. of beans use 30 qts. of water and add 3 tsp. chlorinated lime mixed to a paste with a little water.

4. Drain beans the next morning and pour into sprouting vessel big enough to let them swell three to four times. If a clean flowerpot is used, put a piece of wire netting or cloth across the hole in the bottom. With a milk bottle or fruit jar, cover the opening with a piece of wire screen or cloth, wiring it on after the beans are in the bottle.

5. Keep beans dark and moist. Cover the beans in the flowerpot with a damp cloth. This may then be covered with a piece of damp cardboard to exclude light. If the beans are placed in a wet cloth bag, they should be suspended in a dark, damp place, such as a covered pan with a little water in the bottom; but they should not touch the water. If the beans are not kept dark, they will turn a yellowish green.

6. Water several times daily. The bottom of a flowerpot should be raised slightly so that all water drains out after each watering. With a bottle or jar, simply fill it with water, turning it upside down for the remainder of the time so that the water will drain out and the beans will have air. Each evening it is wise to add a pinch of chlorinated lime to the sprinkling water.

Twenty pounds of beans may be sprouted in this same way. For watering, a spray nozzle on the garden hose may be used, or even better, wire the head of a sprinkling can to the garden hose. The top of the sprouter should be covered with a damp cloth and the beans kept dark. At the last wetting each night, add the chlorinated lime made into a paste to the water that is used for sprinkling. This will prevent the growth of molds and bacteria during the night just as it sterilizes drinking water.

After the second day the sprouting process makes the large quantity of beans warm, and they should be sprinkled with cool water. For additional cooling, a cylinder of wire netting can be placed in the center of the sprouter like a piece of stovepipe. During the last two days, a chunk of ice can be placed on the beans.

The beans are ready to eat from the third to fifth day, but in summer only two days may be needed for sprouting.

Sprouted beans should be kept refrigerated like fresh meat. For longer keeping, they may be blanched for 2 or 3 minutes and then either frozen as is, or fried and frozen.

How to Use Sprouted Soybeans

Use the sprout with bean attached. The beans are chewy but crisp and should not be overcooked. Usual cooking time is only long enough to remove the raw-bean flavor. Many persons prefer to eat them raw. Cooked sprouts can be added to any vegetable combination for casserole dishes, soups, and stews. They are excellent for chop suey dishes. They may be added to salads and to scrambled eggs and omelets.

The beans may be sautéed and served as a plain vegetable. To sauté, place a teaspoon of oil in a pan, add sprouts and a small amount of water, cover, and cook 10 minutes. Some persons prefer only 5 to 8 minutes of cooking. Minced onion browned in the oil gives a good flavor, as does a small amount of soy sauce.

The sprouts may be steamed or cooked a few minutes in water and then browned in a small amount of oil.

Bean Sprout Recipes

⊷ COOKED BEAN SPROUTS

1 lb. fresh bean sprouts
2 tbs. oil
Soy sauce
1 tsp. powdered vegetable broth

Cook bean sprouts in a small amount of water for 3 to 5 minutes. Put oil in heavy pan over moderate flame. Add bean sprouts. Season with powdered vegetable broth and a small amount of soy sauce. Stir until well blended and serve at once. Serves 4.

⊷ STEWED SPROUTS AND TOMATOES

2 cups cooked bean sprouts
1 cup stewed tomatoes

Mix and bring to boil. Add a small amount of margarine and minced parsley. Serve at once. Serves 4 to 6.

⊷ FRIED SPROUTS

1. Fry sprouts in a heavy pan with a small amount of vegetable oil until brown. Stir to prevent burning. Add oil as needed. Sprouts should be crisp and brown in 10 minutes or less.
2. Brown sprouts in oil for 5 minutes, then add a small

amount of water, cover, and cook on low flame for 10
minutes.

3. Brown sprouts and minced onion in oil, add a small
amount of water, season with soy sauce, cover and cook
on low flame until tender.

4. Steam or cook sprouts in water 10 minutes. Then sauté
a few minutes in hot oil. Onions and soy sauce may be
added to flavor.

✍ BEAN SPROUT SOUP

  4 cups clear soup, vegetable broth, or vegetable stock
  2 cups soybean sprouts
  2 beaten eggs

To clear soup, vegetable broth, or stock, add soybean
sprouts. Simmer 8 minutes. Remove from fire and slowly
stir in beaten eggs. Season to taste with salt and vegetable
seasoning. Soy sauce may be added if desired. Serves 6.

✍ SPROUT COLE SLAW

Make cole slaw according to favorite recipe. Add 1 cup
raw soy sprouts.

✍ SPROUTS FOR SALAD

Soy sprouts may be used raw for salads or they may be
cooked 5 minutes, chilled, and mixed with raw and/or
cooked vegetables.

✌ SPROUT COMBINATION SALAD

1 cup slightly cooked sprouts
½ cup chopped celery
4 radishes, sliced
1 cucumber, diced
½ cup green pepper, diced
1 cup shredded lettuce

Mix all together. Chill. Serve on lettuce, topped with green pepper ring and French dressing. Serves 3 to 4.

✌ BEAN SPROUT SUKIYAKI

2 cups vegetable protein food, shredded, or soy cheese
2 tbs. olive oil
2 tbs. food yeast
½ cup green peppers, sliced thin
1 cup sliced celery
1 cup raw bean sprouts
1 large handful spinach
1 cup Chinese cabbage
½ cup green onions, cut into 1½" lengths
1 small can mushrooms
2 tbs. soy sauce
1 tbs. dark brown sugar or honey

Brown vegetable protein food in oil. Add food yeast, and then add the rest of the ingredients except for the spinach. Cover pan tightly, and cook mixture over low heat 12 to 15 minutes. About 3 to 5 minutes before serving, take off the lid and put in the spinach. Replace lid, and cook a few minutes longer. Serve with brown rice. Serves 6 to 8.

Sukiyaki may be cooked at the table in a chafing dish or electric frying pan, or it may be prepared over a barbecue pit. Serve in the container in which it is cooked.

❧ TOSSED SALAD

1 cup shredded lettuce
1 cup grated carrot
1 cup chopped celery
1 cup raw soy sprouts
3 tomatoes, cubed
Watercress

Toss all together, moisten with French dressing or oil, and serve from salad bowl. Serves 4 to 6.

Soy sprouts may be added raw or cooked to any combination of cooked or raw vegetable salad.

❧ BEAN SPROUT CHOP SUEY

¼ cup oil
2 large green peppers, cut in cubes or strips
1 cup onion, cut in thin strips
2 cups celery, cut in diagonal slices
3 cups bean sprouts
1 cup boiling water
2 tbs. flour or cornstarch
1½ tsp. salt
2 tsp. soy sauce

Heat oil in large skillet. Add green peppers, onion, celery, and bean sprouts. Sauté for 2 minutes but do not brown. Add the boiling water. Cover. Cook 5 minutes. Make a paste of the flour, soy sauce, salt, and a little water as needed. Add to the vegetable mixture and cook for 3 minutes. Serve piping hot over noodles or rice. Serves 6.

❧ EGG FOO YONG

  6 eggs
  1 can (4-oz.) mushrooms
  ¼ cup sliced celery
  1 pkg. (10-oz.) French-cut string beans, frozen or fresh
  2 tbs. green onions, chopped
  2 cups fresh bean sprouts
  1 tsp. soy sauce
  ¼ tsp. M.S.G.

Beat eggs, and then add all other ingredients. Drop by tablespoonsful onto hot, lightly oiled griddle. Fry until nicely browned on both sides. Serve with brown gravy. Serves 6.

❧ MIXED CHINESE VEGETABLES

  1 lb. Chinese cabbage (bak choy), shredded, or romaine lettuce
  ½ cup bean sprouts
  ¼ cup sliced mushrooms, fresh or canned
  ½ cup canned bamboo shoots, sliced
  1 tbs. oil
  ¼ cup canned water chestnuts, thinly sliced, or Jerusalem artichokes, sliced, or thin-sliced raw potato
  1 tsp. soy sauce
  ½ tsp. M.S.G.
  Salt to taste.

Mix vegetables lightly and sauté in oil in large fryer, adding more oil if needed. Cook quickly, not over 5 minutes. Add seasoning just before serving. Serves 6.

◆§ SPROUT TOMATO SAUCE

1 cup cooked bean sprouts
2 small onions
2 tbs. oil
½ cup chopped celery
½ cup chopped pepper
2 cups stewed tomatoes
Salt and seasoning as desired

Fry onions in oil until brown, add rest of ingredients, cover, and simmer 10 minutes. Serve over vegetable steaks, cutlets, or loaf. Serves 4.

◆§ BEAN SPROUT CREOLE

4 celery stalks
1 onion
1 clove garlic (optional)
1 tbs. oil
3 cups bean sprouts
1 large can tomatoes
1 tsp. salt
2 bay leaves

Chop celery, onion, and garlic fine. Lightly brown in the oil. Add washed sprouts, tomatoes, salt, and bay leaves. Simmer for 10 minutes. Remove bay leaves. Serve hot or cold. Serves 6.

◆§ SOYBEAN SPROUTS AU GRATIN

3 cups bean sprouts
2 tbs. oil

2 tbs. flour
1 cup milk (soy or dairy)
¾ cup cottage cheese
Salt, paprika
¼ cup oiled bread crumbs

Steam or boil the sprouts 10 minutes. Heat oil over medium flame. Stir in flour. Add milk gradually, stirring constantly until it boils and thickens. Add ½ cup of cheese and the seasoning. Stir until cheese melts. Add sprouts. Pour into greased casserole. Sprinkle with crumbs and rest of cheese. Bake in a moderate oven until brown—20 to 30 minutes. Serves 4 to 6.

⋖§ CHOW MEIN

2 cups soy sprouts
2 cups sliced onion
4 tbs. oil
2 cups shredded vegetable protein food
1 can mushrooms with liquid
2 tbs. soy sauce
Flour or cornstarch for thickening
Seasoning to taste

Cook sprouts 5 minutes. Fry onion in oil until brown; add cooked sprouts, protein food, and chopped mushrooms with liquid. Add water from sprouts, and more water if necessary, to cover. Season as desired and add soy sauce. Thicken mixture with a small amount of flour (whole wheat preferred) or cornstarch, cover, and cook for 5 to 8 minutes. Serve with noodles or rice. Serves 4 to 6.

◄§ SCRAMBLED EGGS WITH BEAN SPROUTS

 ¼ cup onion tops, chopped fine
1½ tsp. salt
 1 to 2 tbs. oil
 4 eggs, slightly beaten
 2 cups raw bean sprouts

Add chopped onion tops and salt to slightly beaten eggs. Let stand 5 to 10 minutes. Wash and sauté bean sprouts 5 minutes in skillet with enough oil to prevent sticking to pan. Add egg mixture and stir. Cook until eggs are scrambled well. Serves 4.

◄§ SPROUT CASSEROLE

2 cups half-cooked sprouts
1 can whole-kernel corn
4 tbs. minced green pepper
1 cup white sauce
Seasoning to taste
Melba toast crumbs

Mix cooked sprouts, corn, and pepper. Season to taste, and almost cover with white sauce. Top with Melba toast crumbs and bake in moderate oven 25 minutes. Serves 4.

◄§ MEATLESS CHOP SUEY

1 cup vegetable burger
2 tbs. oil
1 cup chopped celery
1 small onion, chopped

½ lb. fresh bean sprouts
1 tbs. molasses
2 tbs. soy sauce
Salt
1 tsp. powdered vegetable broth
½ cup water or soup stock

Brown vegetable burger in oil. Add celery, onion, bean sprouts, molasses, soy sauce, salt, and powdered vegetable broth. Add water or soup stock. Mix. Cover and cook slowly for 10 minutes. Serve over brown rice. Serves 3 to 4.

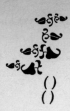

( )
( )

MEAT REPLACEMENT DISHES

Cooked, canned, or ground soybeans and soy grits can be made into delicious loaves, patties, vegetable stuffing, soups, and casserole dishes to be used in place of meat, fish, or poultry.

Soybean Entree Recipes

◆§ COOKED GROUND SOYBEANS

1 cup dry soybeans
1 tsp. salt
Water as needed

Soak the beans overnight in enough salted water to cover them. In the morning, drain, and grind in food chopper, using medium knife. The ground beans resemble creamed corn and may be cooked in a pressure cooker or in an ordinary pan. For pressure cooking, add ½ to 1 cup water, and cook 15 minutes. For ordinary pan, cook after adding 2 to 3 cups water, stirring occasionally, until soft.

⌁ VEGETIZED GROUND SOYBEANS

- 3 tbs. oil
- 2 tbs. onion, minced
- 1 tbs. powdered vegetable broth, or 2 vegetable bouillon cubes
- ½ to 1 cup tomato juice
- 1 tbs. soy sauce or yeast extract flavoring
- 3 cups cooked ground soybeans

Add minced onion to oil, and brown slightly. Add powdered broth, tomato juice, and seasoning, and cook a few minutes. Add ground soybeans. Stir until well blended. Cook over medium flame until almost dry. Serves 4 to 6.

⌁ SOYBURGERS

- 2 eggs
- 2 cups vegetized ground soybeans (see preceding recipe)
- 3 tbs. oil
- 1½ cups wheat germ, bran, or finely crushed Melba toast crumbs

Beat eggs, add vegetized soybeans, and mix in 1 cup wheat germ, bran, or crumbs. Blend thoroughly. Shape as hamburgers or patties, dip in remaining wheat germ, bran, or crumbs, and brown in oil. Serve with brown gravy or tomato sauce, or make into sandwiches.

❧ GROUND SOYBEANS IN GRAVY

Cook ground soybeans until tender. Season as desired and pour into casserole. Almost cover with brown gravy. Bake 20 minutes. Cooked onions are a good addition to this casserole dish.

❧ GROUND SOYBEANS EN CASSEROLE

   3 tbs. oil
   1 cup diced celery
   1 cup sliced onions
   3 cups cooked ground soybeans
   ½ cup whole wheat or soy bread crumbs
   ½ tsp. salt
   Herb or other seasoning as desired (powdered vegetable broth, etc.)
   2 cups tomato pulp

Sauté celery and onions in oil. Mix with ground cooked beans, salt, and other seasoning, and place in casserole. Pour on tomato pulp, top with crumbs, and bake in slow oven 1 to 1½ hours. Serves 6.

❧ SOY LOAVES

Cooked or canned soybeans may be made into loaves, patties, mock sausages, and casserole dishes. The beans may be served plain or with tomato sauce, and may be used whole, mashed, or ground. Always use liquid with canned beans. Ground cooked soybeans may be used in any loaf calling for mashed or ground beans.

৺ SOY LOAF 1

　1　can or 2 cups cooked soybeans
　1　cup cooked celery
　1　cup cooked carrots
　1　sliced tomato
　¼　cup Melba toast crumbs
　1　tbs. powdered vegetable broth

Mash soybeans, and add cooked vegetables, Melba toast crumbs, and vegetable broth. Mix well. Place in buttered loaf pan, top with tomato slices, and bake in hot oven 20 to 30 minutes. Serves 4 to 6.

৺ SOY LOAF 2

　2　cups cooked soybeans
　1　small onion
　1　cup milk (soy or dairy)
　1　egg
　1　tbs. oil
　½　tsp. celery salt
　1　vegetable bouillon cube
　1½　cups Melba toast crumbs or whole wheat crumbs
　½　tsp. sage or thyme

Grind or mash soybeans, and add ground or finely grated onion, beaten egg, and other ingredients. Mix thoroughly and bake in an oiled loaf pan 30 to 40 minutes in a moderate oven. May be served plain or with tomato sauce. Serves 4 to 6.

⋑ SOY LOAF 3

    2 cups soybeans
    1 medium-sized onion
    ½ cup soy toast crumbs
    1 egg
    Salt as desired
    ½ tsp. M.S.G.
    ½ cup tomato soup

Grind beans, onion, and soy toast in food chopper. Beat egg and add ground ingredients. Mix well, adding salt and M.S.G. Add ¼ cup tomato soup and pour mixture into greased loaf pan. Cover top with rest of tomato soup. Bake in moderate oven 40 minutes. Serve with desired sauce or gravy. Serves 4.

As variations, soy or dairy milk may be used instead of tomato soup; and ¼ cup chopped parsley or olives may be added.

⋑ SOY SPINACH LOAF

    2 cups cooked soybeans
    1 cup raw ground spinach
    1 cup chopped celery (cooked or raw)
    ½ cup Melba toast crumbs
    Seasoning as desired (onion, garlic, thyme, sweet basil, etc.)
    1 tbs. vegetable oil

Mash beans, add other ingredients, and mix well. Pour into oiled baking dish and bake 30 minutes in a moderate oven. When done, brush with vegetable oil and serve with tomato sauce. May be baked with sliced tomatoes. Serves 4 to 5.

⋖§ SOY LENTIL LOAF

- 1 cup cooked lentils
- 1 cup cooked soybeans
- 2 cups whole wheat or soy bread crumbs
- 2 tbs. minced parsley
- 2 cups milk (soy or dairy), or 1 cup milk and 1 cup tomato soup
- 1 tbs. powdered vegetable broth, or 1 tsp. poultry seasoning

Mix all ingredients together, pack into oiled loaf pan, and bake in moderate oven 30 to 40 minutes. Serve with brown gravy or tomato sauce. Serves 6.

⋖§ SOY MUSHROOM LOAF

- 2 tbs. oil
- 1 cup diced mushrooms
- 1 tbs. flour
- ½ cup rich soy milk
- 1 egg
- 1 cup bread crumbs
- 2 cups cooked soybeans
- ¼ tsp. salt

Sauté mushroom slightly in oil. Stir in flour and soy milk. Add beaten egg, bread crumbs, soybeans, and salt. Mix thoroughly, place in oiled loaf pan, and bake in moderate oven until brown. Serve with gravy or tomato sauce. Serves 4 to 5.

As variations, 1 cup leftover vegetables may be mixed with soybeans in the above recipe; and tomato or any creamed soup may be used instead of soy milk. If soup is thick, omit flour. Seasonings may be varied to suit different vegetables and tastes.

✿§ SOY RICE LOAF

  2 cups mashed soybeans
  1 cup cooked brown rice
  1 cup milk (soy or dairy)
  ½ cup soy cracker or soy toast crumbs
  1 tbs. oil
  1 tbs. powdered vegetable broth
  2 tbs. minced onion
  Salt as desired

Mix well, and bake in oiled loaf pan in moderate oven for 45 minutes. If desired, moisten top with a little tomato sauce or soup. Serves 4 to 5.

✿§ CANNED SOY ROASTS AND LOAVES

There are any number of excellent soy roasts, loaves, and meat substitute foods on the market that are tasty and ready to use, and can be served hot or cold. The usual method of preparation is to remove the contents from the can by opening both ends and pushing out, then slice and heat. The slices may be fried in oil, breaded, dipped in eggs and fried, heated in gravy or sauce, or broiled. Sliced, they serve as cold cuts or as sandwich fillings, and when mashed they make good sandwich spreads. These foods can be diced and served in cream sauce, à la king. They are also good additions to salads.

✿§ SOYBEANS SOUTHERN STYLE

  2 cups cooked soybeans
  2 cups corn, canned, fresh, or frozen; preferably fresh
  1 cup soy cheese
  2 cups tomatoes, canned or fresh

1 tsp. salt
1 scant cup lightly oiled bread crumbs

Put alternate layers of the beans, corn, soy cheese, and drained tomatoes into a greased baking dish. Mix the salt with the juice drained from the tomatoes and pour over the mixture. Cover with the crumbs and bake in a moderate oven for 30 minutes, or until the crumbs are brown. Serves 8.

◄§ SOYBEANS CREOLE

2 tbs. oil
2 tbs. onion, chopped
4 tbs. green pepper, minced
3 tbs. whole wheat flour
Salt and seasoning to taste
1 cup fresh or canned tomatoes
1 cup brown vegetable stock or broth
2 cups cooked or canned soybeans

Sauté onion and pepper in the oil. Add flour and seasoning and blend well. Add tomatoes and stock and cook 2 or 3 minutes. Add soybeans and simmer 10 minutes. Serve in individual bean pots or ramekins, topped with minced parsley. Serves 4 to 6.

◄§ SOYBEAN CASSEROLE 1

Mix 1 can soybeans plain or with tomato sauce with 2 cups cooked low-starch vegetables, such as carrots, celery, asparagus, or summer squash. Place in casserole and bake 15 minutes in moderate oven. Serve from casserole. Serves 4 to 6.

◆§ SOYBEAN CASSEROLE 2

    2 tbs. oil
    2 cups chopped celery
    4 tbs. chopped onion
    2 tbs. chopped green pepper
    2 cups white sauce
    1 tsp. salt
    2 cups mashed or chopped cooked soybeans
    1 cup whole wheat or soy bread crumbs

Sauté celery, onion, and pepper in a small amount of vegetable oil for 5 minutes. Add white sauce and salt, and bring to boiling point. Add beans and pour mixture into an oiled casserole. Cover with crumbs and bake in moderate oven 45 minutes or until brown. Serve from casserole. Serves 6.

◆§ SOY NUT LOAF

    3 cups cooked soybeans
    2 cups mashed potatoes, hot
    2 cups chopped walnuts
    1 cup milk (soy or dairy)
    1 tbs. yeast extract
    2 tbs. onion, grated
    2 tbs. green pepper, chopped
    2 eggs scrambled to golden brown
    1 raw egg, beaten slightly
    4 tbs. tomato pulp or purée
    Tomato slices
    Parsley

Purée or mash soybeans. Add hot mashed potatoes, nuts, milk, seasonings, scrambled eggs, raw beaten egg, and tomato pulp or purée. Mix lightly. Pour into oiled baking dish and bake slowly 1 hour. Turn baked loaf out onto platter and garnish with sliced tomatoes and parsley. Serve with desired sauce or gravy.

✑ SOY VEGETABLE LOAF

    2 cups cooked soybeans
    ¾ cup cooked carrots
    2 tbs. onion, chopped
    ¾ cup celery
    ¾ cup fresh or canned tomatoes
    1½ tsp. salt
    1½ cups dry bread crumbs

Grind soybeans, carrots, onion, and celery in food chopper. Add tomatoes, salt, and bread crumbs, and mix well. Pack into greased loaf pan. Bake for 45 minutes in moderate oven. May be topped with sliced tomatoes. Serves 4 to 6.

✑ SCALLOPED SOYBEANS

    3 cups cooked soybeans
    1 cup diced celery
    1 small chopped onion
    ½ cup tomato sauce
    ½ tsp. salt
    1 tbs. powdered vegetable broth
    1 cup water or liquid from beans
    2 tbs. oil
    ½ cup whole wheat bread crumbs

Mix all ingredients except crumbs; place in baking dish. Cover with crumbs and bake in moderate oven for 1 to 1½ hours. Serves 6 to 8.

∾§ SOY SAUSAGES

2 cups cooked soybeans
¾ cup whole wheat or Melba toast crumbs
1 egg
½ tsp. salt
2 tsp. vegetable broth
½ tsp. thyme
4 tbs. oil tomato sauce

Mash or grind beans, and add ½ cup crumbs, slightly beaten egg, and seasonings. If mixture seems too dry, add a little milk. Shape into sausages, roll in remaining crumbs, and brown in a small amount of oil. Sausages may be baked in moderate oven. Serve with tomato sauce. Serves 4.

∾§ FRITTERS

2 cups cooked soybeans
2 eggs
1 or 2 tbs. tomato sauce
Salt as desired
2 tsp. powdered vegetable broth

Mash beans and add to beaten eggs. Mix in tomato sauce, a small amount of salt, and powdered vegetable broth. Bake as fritters on a heavy, hot, slightly greased griddle. Serves 6.

∾§ SOY ROAST

1½ cups cooked carrots
1½ cups cooked soybeans
1½ cups cooked beets
½ cup bread crumbs

½ cup tomato juice
1 onion, minced
2 eggs
Thyme or sage and salt to taste

Mash or grind carrots, soybeans, and beets. Add crumbs, tomato juice, minced onion, and beaten eggs. Mix and season to taste. This loaf should be moist; if too dry, add more tomato juice. Place in greased loaf pan, and bake 45 minutes in moderate oven. Serves 6 to 8.

⊷§ SOYBEAN CHOPS

2 cups cooked soybeans
1 cup cooked rice
2 tbs. chopped onion
2 eggs
½ tsp. salt
½ tsp. celery salt
1 cup soft whole wheat bread crumbs (not packed)

Mash soybeans; mix all ingredients together. Form into patties and bake in moderate oven until brown, approximately 45 minutes. Serves 6.

⊷§ PEANUT BUTTER SOY PATTIES

1 cup mashed soybeans
2 tbs. peanut butter
4 tbs. dry bread crumbs

Mix all together. Shape into small patties, roll in Melba toast crumbs, and place in oiled pan. Brown in moderate oven. Serves 4.

◆§ SOYBEAN OMELET

    4 eggs
    2 cups mashed or sieved soybeans
    ½ tsp. salt
    4 tbs. cream or rich soy milk
    Minced parsley

Beat yolks and whites of eggs separately. Add the mashed beans, salt, and cream to the beaten yolks. Fold the whites lightly into the mixture. Pour into a hot buttered baking pan and bake 20 minutes in a quick oven. Serve with minced parsley. Serves 4.

◆§ SOY SOUFFLÉ 1

    3 eggs
    1½ cups mashed or sieved soybeans
    ½ tsp. salt
    1 bouillon cube or 1 tsp. powdered vegetable broth

Beat eggs separately and add soybeans and seasonings to yolks. Fold in beaten whites. Pour into buttered baking dish, and bake in pan of hot water in moderate oven until firm—30 to 45 minutes. Serve hot with mushroom sauce. Serves 4.

As a variation, add 1 tbs. minced onion and/or 2 tbs. chopped parsley.

◆§ SOY SOUFFLÉ 2 (No Eggs)

    1 cup dry soybeans
    4 cups water

2 tbs. oil
1 or 2 tsp. salt
1 tsp. M.S.G.
1 tsp. mixed herbs, as summer savory with sweet basil
1½ cups hot tomato or mushroom sauce

Soak soybeans in 3 cups water overnight. Next morning, remove from water, grind, and add back enough water to make 5 cups pulp. Beans may be run in liquefier; if so, use water in liquefying. Add oil, salt, M.S.G., and herbs. Pour mixture into shallow pan to depth of 2", and bake in slow oven for 1½ to 2 hours until firmly set. Cut in squares and serve with sauce. Serves 8.

The soufflé may be cooled and mixed with celery and mayonnaise as a delicious sandwich or toast spread. It may also be sliced and served alone.

◄§ STUFFED PEPPERS

6 to 8 green peppers
2 cups mashed soybeans
¼ cup minced onion
½ cup finely chopped celery
¼ cup tomato sauce or tomato pulp
½ cup finely shredded carrot
1½ cups oiled bread crumbs

Remove seeds and partitions from inside of green peppers. Boil 3 minutes, drain, and sprinkle inside with salt. Fill with mixture of mashed soybeans, onion, celery, and carrot moistened with tomato sauce. Top with crumbs and bake 30 minutes or until peppers are soft. Serves 6 to 8.

❧ QUICK PATTIES

> 2 cups cooked soybeans
> 1 small onion
> ½ cup soy crackers or bread crumbs
> 1 egg
> ½ tsp. M.S.G.
> Tomato sauce

Grind beans, onion, and crackers or bread in food chopper. Add mixture to beaten egg. Add M.S.G. Drop 1 tbs. or more of mixture on a hot oiled griddle. Brown on both sides. Serve hot with tomato sauce. Serves 4 or 5.

❧ STUFFED TOMATOES

> 6 firm tomatoes
> 2 cups mashed soybeans
> 1 cup cooked celery
> 1 tsp. minced green pepper
> 1 tsp. minced onion
> Desired seasoning
> Oiled bread crumbs

Remove pulp from tomatoes, and sprinkle inside with salt. Mix soybeans, celery, pepper, onion, and seasoning with tomato pulp. Fill tomatoes with mixture, top with oiled crumbs, and bake in moderate oven 30 minutes or until tomatoes are soft. Serves 6.

Soybean Grits or Bits Recipes

Soybean grits, or quick-cooking cracked soybeans as they are often called, make excellent meat replacement dishes, loaves, and patties. The cooked grits may be used as cooked bean pulp or mashed beans. For meatlike flavor, add soy sauce or desired yeast extract seasonings. The grits may be coarse, medium, or fine. Puffed grits may also be used.

✑ COOKED SOY GRITS

Cook soy grits as for cereal. They swell to almost three times their volume, and require only 3 to 5 minutes cooking. For loaves and patties, have cooked grits as dry as possible. The basic rule is:

    1 cup grits
    2 cups water
    ½ tsp. salt

Add grits to boiling salted water. Cook over low flame until dry, stirring occasionally to prevent burning. Grits are now ready to use in several different ways as loaves, patties, and casserole dishes, and may be substituted for the mashed soybeans in any of the above recipes.

✑ SOY GRITS LOAF 1 (No Eggs)

    2 cups cooked soy grits
    1 tbs. powdered vegetable broth or desired seasoning
    2 tbs. minced parsley
    1 tbs. minced onion
    1 cup Melba toast crumbs
    ½ cup tomato juice or soup

Mix grits, seasonings, and crumbs together and pack into baking pan. Moisten top with tomato juice or soup and bake until brown. Serve hot or cold. Serves 4.

◄§ SOY GRITS LOAF 2

1 cup grits
1 tsp. salt
2 cups water
½ cup whole wheat bread crumbs
1 small onion
1 tbs. vegetable seasoning
2 eggs
½ cup milk (soy or dairy)

Cook grits with salt in boiling water until dry. Run crumbs and onion through food chopper. Add to cooked grits with seasoning, beaten eggs, and milk. Mix well. Place in loaf pan and bake 1 hour in moderate oven. Serves 4 to 6.

This mixture may be used for patties. Brown in a small amount of fat, or brush lightly with oil and bake in hot oven until brown.

◄§ VEGETIZED SOY GRITS

2 cups cooked grits
3 tbs. oil
1½ tbs. powdered vegetable broth
1 tbs. soy sauce
½ cup water

Have cooked grits as dry as possible. Add to the following sauce, and serve immediately when well browned.

Add broth, soy sauce, and water to oil. Boil 1 minute. Add cooked grits and cook until well browned. Stir constantly. Serve hot with vegetables.

As variations, onions, celery, and other vegetables may be added; and celery salt, bouillon cubes, and the like may be used instead of powdered vegetable broth.

✍ SOY VEGETABLE HASH

    2 cups cooked grits
    2 cups cooked low-starch vegetables, such as celery, car-
      rots, or summer squash
    ½ cup minced olives
    1 tbs. powdered vegetable
    2 tsp. yeast extract
    Tomato slices

Mix all except tomato slices together. Pour into shallow pan, cover with sliced tomatoes, and bake in hot oven until brown. Serves 4 to 6.

✍ SOY VEGETABLE MULLIGAN

This is an excellent inexpensive dish and can be made with any vegetable desired. Here is one suggestion:

    6 cups boiling water
    1 small bunch celery, chopped
    4 carrots, diced
    1 rutabaga, diced
    1 turnip, diced
    1 large celery root, diced
    3 or 4 sprays parsley
    1 medium-sized onion, diced
    ½ cup soy grits
    1 small can green peas
    1 tbs. soy sauce or other seasoning
    Salt to taste

To boiling water, add next 8 ingredients, and cook until vegetables are tender. Add peas and soy sauce or other seasoning. Serves 6 to 8.

Oil may be added for extra richness. Canned soybeans may be used in place of the grits.

⊷ ZUCCHINI CASSEROLE

    3 cups sliced zucchini
    6 tbs. uncooked soy grits, regular or puffed
    1 tsp. salt
    1 can tomato soup

Wash and slice zucchini; do not peel. Put in layers in casserole, sprinkling each layer with soy grits and a little salt. Fill casserole and top with a few grits. Pour in tomato soup, adding water if necessary to cover. Cover and bake in moderate oven until done, about 1 hour. Remove cover for last 15 minutes to brown. Do not have casserole too full, because grits swell. Serves 6.

As variations, minced onion may be added; this recipe may be made with any vegetable; and milk, soup stock, cream soup, or white sauce may be used in place of tomato soup.

⊷ EGGPLANT CASSEROLE

    1 eggplant, peeled and diced
    1 green pepper, chopped
    1 small onion, chopped
    ⅓ cup uncooked soy grits
    2 cups stewed or canned tomatoes
    Seasoning to taste

Place a layer of diced eggplant in casserole. Top with layer of green pepper and onion and sprinkle on the soy grits. Top with rest of eggplant, pepper, and onion. Add tomatoes. Cover and bake 40 minutes in a moderate oven. Serves 4 to 6.

✑ STUFFED CABBAGE LEAVES

1 cup cooked soy grits
1 tbs. oil
Salt and other seasoning to taste
1 tbs. soy sauce or meatlike flavoring
½ cup minced ripe olives
1 head slightly wilted cabbage, well washed
Water or tomato juice
Gravy or tomato sauce

Soy grits should be as dry as possible. To them add oil, desired amount of salt and other seasoning, soy sauce or meatlike flavoring, and minced ripe olives. Mix well and use to fill center of cabbage leaves. Close ends of each leaf and pin together with toothpick. Place in shallow oiled pan, add a small amount of water or tomato juice, and bake in moderate oven until leaves are done, about 20 minutes. Serve hot with gravy or sauce. Serves 4 to 6.

✑ SOY GRITS CROQUETTES 1

2 tbs. minced onions
¾ cup stewed tomatoes
2 tbs. soy flour
1 cup cooked diced celery
2 cups cooked soy grits
Melba toast crumbs

Add minced onion to tomatoes. Bring to boil, add soy flour, and cook until thick. Cool. Add celery and soy grits. Mix well and shape into croquettes. Dip in Melba toast crumbs and bake on oiled tin in moderate oven 20 minutes. Serve with gravy or sauce. Serves 4 to 6.

✒ SOY GRITS CROQUETTES 2

1 tbs. oil
2 cups cooked grits
1 cup cooked brown rice
5 tbs. minced onion
½ tsp. salt
1 tbs. powdered vegetable broth
Other seasoning to taste
½ cup cornmeal bread or cracker crumbs
1 egg

Brown onion in oil. Add cooked grits, rice, and seasoning. Mold into croquettes, dip in beaten egg, then in corn meal or crumbs. Place in shallow greased pan and bake in hot oven about 30 minutes or until brown. Serve with gravy or tomato sauce. Serves 6.

✒ SOY GRITS PATTIES (No Egg)

2 cups cooked soy grits
1 tbs. powdered vegetable broth
1 or 2 tsp. yeast extract
1 tbs. oil
Melba toast crumbs

Have cooked grits as dry as possible. While hot add oil, powdered vegetable broth, and yeast extract. Mix well. Drop by spoonsful into finely crushed Melba toast crumbs. Cover well. Handle as little as possible and shape into patties. Place on oiled tin and bake in hot oven until brown. They will hold their shape when baked. Serve with tomato sauce. Serves 4 to 5.

‹§ SOY EGGPLANT PATTIES

1 eggplant, peeled and diced
Salt to taste
Powdered vegetable broth to taste
Soy sauce to taste
2 cups cooked soy grits
Melba toast crumbs
Gravy or tomato sauce

The eggplant acts as a binder in this recipe. Steam or cook eggplant until tender. Mash and add seasonings as desired. Work in cooked soy grits, which should be as dry as possible; the amount of grits will vary with the size of the eggplant. Mix well, and shape into patties. Roll in crumbs, and bake on oiled tin until brown. Serve with gravy or tomato sauce. Serves 4 to 6.

As a variation, a nut patty may be made by using ground almonds in place of soy grits, or use 1 cup nuts and 1 cup cooked soy grits.

‹§ SOY GRITS FRITTERS

1 cup cooked soy grits
½ tsp. salt
2 eggs
1 tbs. soy sauce
Vegetable seasoning if desired

Add grits and salt to beaten eggs and soy sauce. Mix well. Drop from tablespoon onto a hot greased griddle. Do not turn until well browned on one side. Make these cakes quite thick. Serve hot with sauce or gravy. Serves 4 to 6.

⋖§ SCRAMBLED EGGS AND SOY PUFFS

   4 eggs
½ cup milk (soy or dairy)
   4 tbs. puffed soy grits
¼ tsp. salt
1½ tbs. oil
Parsley

Beat eggs slightly until yolks and whites are blended; add milk, puffs, and salt. Put oil in heavy skillet, turn in egg mixture, and cook at a low temperature until creamy, scraping the cooked portion from the sides of the pan so that the uncooked part will reach the bottom. When done, remove from pan to hot platter, and serve immediately. Garnish with parsley. Serves 4 to 5.

⋖§ SOY GRITS OMELET

   4 egg yolks
¼ cup uncooked soy grits, mixed with ¼ cup water
½ tsp. salt
   4 egg whites plus 4 tbs. water
   2 tbs. oil

Beat egg yolks until fluffy. Add soaked soy grits and blend thoroughly. Add salt and water to egg whites and beat until stiff. Fold in yolk mixture and pour into skillet containing the hot oil. Cover and cook slowly over a low flame until set around edges. Remove cover, place in moderate oven for 15 minutes to complete cooking, and allow to brown slightly on top. Fold over and serve. Serves 4.

⋖§ SOY FRENCH OMELET

     4 eggs
   ¾ cup milk (soy or dairy)
   ¼ tsp. salt
     4 tbs. puffed soy grits

Beat eggs slightly until yolks and whites are blended. Add milk, salt, and grits. Pour mixture into a heavy, dry, hot pan, stirring constantly until mixture is the consistency of a soft custard. Remove at once from pan, and serve. Serves 4 to 5.

⋖§ CASHEW LOAF

   1½ cups ground cashews
     1 medium onion, chopped and sautéed in 1½ tbs. oil
   ½ cup dry bread crumbs
     1 cup vegetable burger
     1 cup cooked rice
     1 cup soy milk
     1 tsp. parsley
     1 tsp. paprika
     1 tsp. smoked flavoring
   ¼ tsp. powdered thyme, or ½ tsp. thyme leaf
   ½ tsp. M.S.G.
     Salt to taste

Put all ingredients into bowl in order listed. Mix thoroughly and salt to taste. Let stand for 10 or 15 minutes, and then pack firmly into well-oiled loaf pan. Bake for 40 to 50 minutes in moderate oven. Serves 8 generously.

Serve with your favorite gravy or sauce. Cashew loaf is delicious served cold with homemade catsup. It also freezes well.

◄§ RICE PILAFF

   1 can (4-oz.) mushroom pieces
   4 green onions, chopped
  ½ cup soy grits
   1 cup uncooked long-grained brown rice
  ½ tsp. oregano
   2 tbs. oil
   2 small pkgs. George Washington broth powder
   4 cups water

Sauté mushrooms, onions, soy grits, rice, and oregano in the oil until brown. Add broth powder and water, and put all into a covered casserole. Bake covered for 1 hour in moderate oven. This is easily reheated, and so may be made the day before. Serves 4 to 6.

◄§ SOYBEAN LOAF

   2 cups cooked soybeans, mashed
  ½ cup whole wheat bread crumbs
   1 tbs. oil
   1 onion, minced
   1 tsp. salt
   2 tbs. soy flour
  ½ cup minced olives

Mix ingredients well. Let stand ½ hour in oiled baking dish. Bake 35 to 40 minutes in moderate oven. May be served with gravy. Serves 4 to 6.

Bean pulp left from making soy cheese may be used instead of mashed beans.

❧ CURRIED VEGETABLE CUTLETS

  2 tbs. oil
  1 tbs. onion, chopped
  ½ tsp. orange rind, grated
  1 bay leaf
  Sprinkle of garlic salt, ground coriander seed, turmeric,
    cumin, celery salt
  4 tbs. flour
  1 tsp. salt
  1 cup soy milk
  2 cups coconut cream
  1 can (20-oz.) vegetable cutlets
  Few slices onion
  3 tbs. chopped parsley
  1 pkg. George Washington Broth-Golden, or 1 tsp. Mc-
    Kay's vegetable chicken flavoring
  4 to 6 cups cooked brown rice or noodles

Put oil in fryer, add onion and seasonings, and sauté lightly. Then add flour and salt, mix smooth, and add soy milk slowly. Put this mixture in double boiler and slowly add coconut milk. Cook until thick. Drain liquid from vegetable cutlets, and cut each cutlet into 5 strips. Put into pan with enough water just to cover, add a few slices of onion, chopped parsley, and George Washington broth or McKay's vegetable chicken flavoring. Stew slowly while sauce is cooking. Just before serving, combine sauce and vegetable cutlets. Serve over hot brown rice or noodles. Serves 6 to 8.

Pass a tray with small dishes containing chopped roasted peanuts, chopped green onions, chopped cashews, chutney and chopped coconut chips or shredded toasted coconut.

✑ SOY GRITS CASSEROLE

    2 cups cooked soy grits
    1 cup cooked carrots
    1 cup cooked celery
    2 tbs. minced parsley
    1 cup stewed tomatoes
    2 tbs. powdered vegetable broth
    1 cup Melba toast crumbs

Mix all except crumbs together, pour into buttered casserole, top with crumbs, and bake until brown. Serves 6 to 8.

✑ MEATLESS CHILI

    ½ cup chopped onions
    4 tbs. vegetable oil
    1 medium can vegetable protein, diced
    ¼ tsp. cumin
    ½ tsp. oregano
    2 cups cooked soybeans
    2 cups tomatoes, canned or fresh
    Soy sauce or meatlike flavoring

Cook onions in oil until brown. Add vegetable protein food and seasonings. Stir, and add beans, tomatoes, and soy sauce. Bring to the boiling point. Serves 4 to 5.

✑ OVEN CROQUETTES

    2 tbs. chopped onion
    1½ cups chopped celery
    1 cup puréed tomato
    1 tsp. salt
    4 tbs. flour

2 tbs. oil
3 cups soybean pulp
Breadcrumbs or cornflakes
1 beaten egg
2 tbs. milk

Mix together onion, celery, puréed tomato and salt. Blend flour and oil. Bring tomato mixture to a boil, then add slowly to flour blend, stirring until smooth. Return to stove and cook slowly, stirring, until thickened and smooth. Cool. Add soybean pulp and roll into croquettes of desired size. Dip each croquette into blended egg and milk, then into crumbs or cornflakes. Bake in hot oven for about 30 minutes. Serves 6 to 8.

SOY NOODLES, MACARONI, AND SPAGHETTI

Recently the soybean has made its appearance in the form of soy noodles, macaroni, spaghetti, and other pasta products. They are not made entirely from soy flour but are mixed with whole wheat or white flour. Those made with whole wheat flour are darker in color. Both taste good and have become popular. Some are vegetized, having added vegetables like carrots or tomatoes.

Soy macaroni and noodles may be cooked and used like any wheat or egg noodles. They are delicious in soups and in casserole dishes, served with tomato sauce or cheese. The recipes below serve very well as the main protein dish of the meal.

Soy Pasta Recipes

⋅⅋ SOY NOODLES AND MUSHROOMS 1

2 cups soy noodles
1 can mushroom pieces
Seasoning
Milk (soy or dairy)

Cook noodles according to package directions, drain, and place in casserole. Add mushroom pieces and seasoning, and enough milk to almost cover. Bake in a moderate oven 30 minutes. Serves 4.

⋅⅋ SOY NOODLES AND MUSHROOMS 2

2 cups soy noodles
1 can cream of mushroom soup
Seasoning if desired
Milk (soy or dairy)
Whole wheat bread crumbs

Cook noodles according to package directions, drain, and place in casserole. Cover with cream of mushroom soup; if not enough to cover, add milk. Top with crumbs and bake in moderate oven 30 minutes. Serves 4.

Macaroni or spaghetti may be used in place of noodles.

⋅⅋ SOY MACARONI AND ALMONDS

1 cup soy macaroni
1 cup milk (soy or dairy)
½ tsp. salt
2 tbs. oil

2 tbs. whole wheat flour
¾ cup almonds, shredded

Boil macaroni in salted water until done, but not mushy;
drain. Make a white sauce from milk, oil, salt, and whole
wheat flour. Add ½ cup almonds to sauce. Place macaroni
in buttered casserole and pour sauce over it. Sprinkle with
¼ cup almonds and bake until brown in moderate oven.
Serves 4.

As a variation, add 1 to 2 cups thinly sliced vegetable
cutlets or steaks.

◄§ SOY MACARONI AND CHEESE

2 cups soy macaroni
1 cup cottage cheese
1 cup white sauce
½ cup Melba toast crumbs or soy grits

Cook macaroni in salted water; drain. Layer in casserole
and top each layer with cottage cheese. Cover with white
sauce, top with Melba toast crumbs or soy grits, and bake
30 minutes in moderate oven. Serves 4 to 6.

◄§ SOY MACARONI AND CELERY

2 cups cooked soy macaroni
2 cups cooked celery
1½ cups white sauce
2 tsp. powdered vegetable broth
Other seasonings as desired
Toast crumbs

Mix macaroni and celery. Add white sauce and seasonings. Pour into casserole, top with crumbs, and bake in moderate oven 20 to 30 minutes. Serves 4 to 5.

As variations, add or top with desired amount of soy cheese; or add soy sauce or yeast extract seasoning. Use carrots, spinach, and other low-starch vegetables instead of celery; use lima beans, soybeans, lentils, or peas instead of macaroni; and use brown gravy or mushroom soup instead of white sauce.

◄§ SOY MACARONI LOAF

    1 cup cooked soy macaroni
    3 cups cooked soybeans
    1 egg
    3 or 4 tbs. onion, grated
    ¼ cup tomato soup or sauce
    Salt and seasoning as desired

Cook macaroni in salted water and drain. Grind soybeans in food chopper. Beat egg well and add all ingredients. Mix thoroughly. Bake in oiled loaf pan in moderate oven 40 minutes. Serves 4 to 5.

◄§ QUICK SOY SPAGHETTI

    2 cups soy sphaghetti
    1 can tomato soup or sauce
    Minced parsley

Cook soy spaghetti in salted water until tender; drain. Add to hot, undiluted tomato soup. Sprinkle with minced parsley and serve at once. Tomato sauce may be used instead of soup. Serves 4 to 6.

As a variation, add 1 cup of any ground gluten product.

৩ SOY MACARONI CHEESE LOAF

¾ cup soy macaroni
1 tbs. parsley, chopped
2 tbs. onion, chopped
2 tbs. oil
1 cup soy cheese or cottage cheese
1½ cups milk (soy or dairy)
1 egg
1 tsp. salt
½ cup oiled crumbs

Cook macaroni in salted water until tender. Cook parsley and onion in oil until soft. Place a layer of drained macaroni in baking dish and add a layer of onion and soy or cottage cheese. When dish is full, pour in milk mixed with beaten egg and salt. Cover with bread crumbs and bake in moderate oven until brown and set—about 30 minutes. Serves 4.

৩ SOY SPAGHETTI AND CHEESE

1 cup cooked soy spaghetti
1 cup soy cheese, mashed
2 tbs. onion, grated
1 egg, hard-cooked and cut fine
1 cup soy milk
3 tbs. bread crumbs

Place spaghetti and cheese in layers in casserole. Add onion and egg. Pour soy milk over this, and sprinkle top with bread crumbs. Bake 30 minutes in moderate oven. Serves 2 or 3.

Pimiento may be added, and macaroni may be substituted for spaghetti.

CREOLE SPAGHETTI

2 cups soy spaghetti
2 cups vegetable protein food
1 medium-sized green pepper, diced
1 medium-sized onion, diced
4 tbs. oil
2 cups stewed tomatoes
Salt and seasoning to taste

Cook spaghetti in salted water and drain. Chop vegetable protein food. Sauté onion and pepper in fat for a few minutes. Add vegetable protein food and brown. Add tomatoes, spaghetti, salt, and seasoning; cover, and cook 15 to 20 minutes, stirring frequently. Serves 4 to 6.

SOY SPAGHETTI AND VEGETABLE SAUCE

1 pkg. (8-oz.) soy spaghetti
2 tbs. olive oil
1 can (2-oz.) mushrooms (drain and save liquid)
½ cup pine nuts, whole
½ green pepper, thinly sliced
½ cup walnuts, mashed or ground
2 cups any commercial vegetable protein cutlets or steaks
    cut into small pieces
1 can tomato paste
1 cup liquid, part mushroom liquid and rest water
4 tbs. soy sauce
½ tsp. oregano
1 tsp. paprika
1 tsp. mixed herbs
½ tsp. cumin
1 tsp. M.S.G.
Salt to taste

Put spaghetti on to boil in salted water. Put next three ingredients in large, heavy fryer, sauté until tender, and add next three ingredients and cook a few minutes, stirring. Add remainder of ingredients and seasoning. Cook slowly at least 15 minutes. Drain spaghetti, and combine with sauce. Serves 6.

Ground almonds may be substituted for pine nuts, but the nuts are better.

◆§ SOY SPAGHETTI WITH VEGETABLE BURGER

1 pkg. (8-oz.) soy and whole wheat spaghetti
3 tbs. vegetable oil
⅓ cup onion, chopped
½ cup green pepper, chopped
1 cup chopped celery
1 can (8-oz.) mushrooms (drain and save liquid)
1 tbs. soy sauce
2 cans (6-oz. ea.) tomato paste
Liquid from canned mushrooms
1½ cups vegetable burger
1 tsp. salt
⅛ tsp. garlic powder
1 tsp. leaf oregano
⅛ tsp. ground cumin
Chopped parsley

Put spaghetti on to boil in salted water. Put next six ingredients in heavy kettle or fryer, and cook slowly until onion is clear. Add vegetable burger, and cook 5 minutes. Add tomato paste, mushroom liquid, and seasonings. Cook slowly 10 minutes. Drain spaghetti, and pour half the sauce over it; mix lightly. Serve on platter. Garnish top with remaining sauce and chopped parsley. Serves 8 generously.

SAUCES
AND GRAVIES

The recipes below, some of them mentioned as part of the dishes described in this book, are delicious additions to many main courses and vegetables.

Sauce Recipes

⊷ QUICK TOMATO SAUCE

Heat can of tomato soup diluted with ¼ to ½ cup water. Serve as sauce.

⊷ TOMATO SAUCE 1

4 large ripe tomatoes, peeled
1 tbs. celery salt
4 tbs. parsley, chopped fine
4 tbs. celery, chopped fine
1 tbs. lemon juice

4 tbs. green peppers, chopped fine
2 tbs. brown sugar or honey

Place all ingredients in covered saucepan and cook slowly until mixture thickens. Stir occasionally to prevent scorching.

◄§ TOMATO SAUCE 2

1 can or 2 cups stewed tomatoes
1 onion, sliced
2 stalks celery, chopped
¼ bunch parsley, chopped
Salt and desired seasoning
2 tbs. oil
1 tbs. whole wheat flour

Boil first five ingredients 20 minutes, remove from fire, and strain through sieve. Mix oil and flour in skillet over medium flame; brown. Add tomato mixture and cook a few minutes until thick.

◄§ TOMATO SAUCE WITH ONION AND PEPPER

1 medium-sized onion, grated fine
½ green pepper, shredded
2 tbs. oil
½ tsp. salt
1 tsp. powdered vegetable broth
1 tbs. yeast extract
1 can (No. 2) tomatoes, put through sieve

Mix onion and pepper in heavy pan, adding oil, salt, and powdered vegetable broth. Cook until slightly brown.

Add yeast extract and tomatoes. Cover and cook over low to medium flame until thick.

Diced mushrooms and minced olives are good additions.

✑ TOMATO CATSUP

4 qts. ripe tomatoes, quartered
2 red sweet peppers, cut in strips
2 green peppers, cut in strips
1 cup celery, cut in 1" pieces
1 cup onions, coarsely chopped
1 bay leaf
1 tbs. celery seed
1 tbs. coriander seed
2 tbs. salt, or to taste
2 cups lemon juice (do not strain, but take out seeds)
½ cup brown sugar

Put tomatoes, peppers, celery, and onions in a blender jar (about ¾ full) and blend at high speed for 4 to 6 seconds, or until liquefied. Pour into large kettle. Repeat until all vegetables are used. Tie bay leaf and seeds in muslin cloth and add to tomato mixture. Cook in slow oven or electric saucepan until reduced to about ½ the original volume. Add lemon juice and sugar, and cook a few minutes longer until desired consistency. Seal immediately in hot sterile jars. Makes 4 to 6 pints. Will keep in the refrigerator for several weeks.

If you do not have a blender, cut vegetables finer and cook until tender. Then put through a sieve or food mill and add seasoning. Cook down to ½ the original volume. Add lemon juice and sugar last, but be sure it has cooked at least 5 minutes before canning. Will make a little less than with the blender method.

◆§ TOMATO RELISH

   1 lb. onions, diced fine
   1 medium bunch celery, diced fine
   1 qt. raw tomatoes, ripe or green
   1 tbs. brown sugar
   Juice of two lemons
   2 bay leaves
   Pinch of sweet basil
   1 tsp. salt

Cook onion and celery together in a small amount of water, or without water if possible. When about half done, add tomatoes, sugar, lemon juice, and seasonings. Simmer together until vegetables are tender and flavors are blended. Remove bay leaves. This relish may be canned in small jars for future use. Keep handy to serve with loaves, patties, in sandwiches, or with plain cooked legumes.

This relish may also be cooked in an electric fryer, in the oven, or on a controlled burner. It will not then require as close watching.

◆§ VEGETIZED SAUCE

   1 tbs. oil
   1 tbs. powdered vegetable broth
   1 tsp. yeast extract paste
   ¼ to ½ cup water

Mix oil, powdered vegetable broth, and paste together well. Add water, stirring constantly. Cook a few minutes.

Pour over meat substitute, or heat vegetables or soybeans in this sauce. Very good on new potatoes.

✑ BASIC WHITE SAUCE, WITH VARIATIONS

    2 tbs. oil
    2 tbs. flour (whole wheat preferred)
    ¼ tsp. salt
    1 cup milk (soy or dairy)

Put oil into double boiler. Add flour and blend well. Add salt and milk; cook, stirring constantly, until thick. Cover and cook in double boiler 10 minutes.

Variations:

Thin sauce: 1 tbs. oil and 1 tbs. flour to 1 cup milk.

Thick sauce: 4 tbs. oil and 4 tbs. flour to 1 cup of milk.

Brown sauce: brown flour and fat well. Add a small amount of soy sauce or yeast paste.

Egg sauce: stir 1 beaten raw egg, scrambled egg, or chopped hard-cooked egg into white sauce.

Olive sauce: add 4 tbs. minced ripe olives to sauce.

Parsley sauce: add desired amount of minced parsley to sauce.

Mushroom sauce: add ¼ cup chopped mushrooms to sauce.

✑ YEAST PASTE

    1 cup baker's or food yeast
    4 tbs. soy sauce
    ⅔ cup water
    1 tsp. powdered vegetable broth, or ½ tsp. celery salt
    ½ tsp. onion salt

Mix and cook over low flame, stirring constantly until thick. Pour into small jar, cover, and use as needed. Keep in refrigerator. This resembles the commercial meatlike pastes.

Gravy Recipes

⮧ BROWN GRAVY

2 tbs. oil
2 tbs. whole wheat flour
1 cup cold water
1 tbs. soy sauce or ½ tbs. yeast extract
Salt to taste

Mix oil, flour, and soy sauce or yeast extract and cook until brown. Add cold water, stirring constantly, until gravy is smooth and thickened. Correct seasoning.

As variations, 1 tsp. powdered vegetable broth gives a nice flavor; or add 1 to 2 tbs. chopped mushrooms.

⮧ MUSHROOM GRAVY

1 can (8-oz.) mushroom soup
1 tbs. oil
1½ tsp. flour
1 tbs. parsley, minced

Heat soup. Blend oil and flour; add hot soup to make a cream sauce. Stir constantly. Add minced parsley and serve at once. Add more water or milk to make right consistency.

✺ MOCK GIBLET GRAVY

    1 can (4-oz.) mushrooms chopped (drain and save liquid)
    ½ cup chopped gluten product
    2 tbs. oil
    4 tbs. flour
2½ cups liquid (include mushroom liquid)
    2 tbs. chopped parsley
    2 tsp. vegetable chicken flavoring
    Salt to taste

Brown mushrooms and gluten bits in oil until quite brown. Add flour, stir and brown lightly, and then add liquid. Stir constantly until thick. Add seasonings, and salt to taste.

✺ BOUILLON GRAVY

    2 tbs. oil
    1 tbs. minced onion
    2 tbs. whole wheat flour
    1 vegetable bouillon cube
    1 cup water
    Seasoning as desired

Add minced onion to oil and cook a few minutes. Blend in flour. Add bouillon dissolved in water and cook, stirring constantly until thickened. Season as desired.

✺ BROWN EGG GRAVY

    4 tbs. oil
    1 egg beaten to a foam
    ¼ cup browned flour

2 cups milk (soy or dairy)
½ tsp. salt

Put oil in skillet. When fairly hot, add beaten egg. Stir constantly until egg particles are browned. Add browned flour, and stir until smooth. Gradually add milk, stirring constantly. Add salt and other seasoning if desired. Bring to boiling point and serve.

◂§ CASHEW GRAVY

1 cup water
Salt to taste
¼ cup raw cashews
½ tsp. smoked flavoring

Liquefy all together and cook until thick. Add 2 to 4 tbs. chopped mushrooms if desired.

SOY SOUPS

Soy soups may be made from the whole beans, ground or mashed beans, soy grits, soy flour, soy milk, and soy milk powder. If possible, cook soups made with dried beans in a pressure cooker. Soaked and ground dried beans may be used for long-cooking soups, and if partly cooked may be added to vegetable soups. Soy grits and flour can be added just before serving, and are a quick way to add protein to any soup. The grits, being almost starchless, are preferred to rice and barley for a low-starch diet. Soy milk may be used for cream soup, and soy milk powder or the low-fat flour may be mixed with water and used in place of liquid soy milk. Smooth cream and purée soups are quickly made in a liquefier, and fortunate is the cook who owns one.

General Soup Rule (*U. S. Department of Agriculture*)
To add soy flour to any vegetable soups, use ¼ cup soy flour to each quart (4 cups) of soup. Blend the flour with

an equal amount of stock, and add to the soup for a few minutes' cooking before serving.

Soy Soup Recipes

◆§ PURÉE OF SOY SOUP

    1 cup cooked or canned soybeans
    1 tbs. whole wheat flour
 2½ cups milk (soy or dairy) or vegetable stock
    1 tbs. oil
    1 tsp. salt
    1 tbs. powdered vegetable broth
    3 cups hot water

Mashed soybeans may be added to milk or vegetable stock. Press soybeans through a sieve or liquefy. Make a sauce of flour, milk or stock, oil, salt, and powdered vegetable broth. Add mashed soybeans and hot water to sauce. Serve with whole-grain or soy crackers, or toast strips. Serves 6.

◆§ CREAM OF SOY SOUP

    2 cups cooked soybeans
    3 cups milk (soy or dairy)
    Salt to taste
    Sprinkling of minced parsley or alfalfa sprouts

Mash or sieve soybeans. Add milk and a little salt. Serve hot, topped with minced parsley or alfalfa sprouts. Serves 4.

✑ QUICK SOY SOUP

3 vegetable bouillon cubes
3 cups water
Seasoning as desired
1 cup mashed cooked or canned soybeans

Pour boiling water over bouillon cubes; add mashed soybeans and desired seasoning. Part milk and part water may
be used. Serves 3.

✑ SOY ONION SOUP

1 cup dry soybeans
4 cups water
3 onions, quartered
1 tbs. soy sauce
1 tbs. powdered vegetable broth

Wash beans and soak them overnight in 3 cups salted water. Add onions to soaked beans with 1 cup water and seasoning, and cook in pressure cooker 1 hour. Run through
sieve. Add water as desired for thick or thin soup. Add seasoning to taste. Serves 4 to 6.

Celery or a mixture of celery and onions may be used in
place of onions.

✑ VEGETABLE SOY SOUP

1 cup diced carrots
1 small stalk celery, chopped
1 qt. salted water
1 cup mashed soybeans
1 tbs. powdered vegetable broth
Sprinkling of minced parsley

Cook carrots and celery in salted water until very tender. When done, add mashed soybeans and powdered vegetable broth. Run through sieve or liquefy. Serve hot with minced parsley. Serves 6.

⮜§ SOY GRITS SOUP

Follow favorite pea or lentil soup recipe, using tenderized or quick-cooking soybeans or soy grits instead of peas or lentils. A small amount of soy grits may be added to any soup a few minutes before serving.

⮜§ SOY GRITS VEGETABLE SOUP

    1 qt. water
    ½ cup peas, shelled
    1 cup celery, chopped
    ½ cup carrots, grated
    ½ cup turnips, diced
    1 medium onion, chopped
    2 or 3 tbs. soy grits
    1 tsp. salt
    2 tsp. powdered vegetable broth
    Other seasonings as desired

Add vegetables to water and cook until tender. When done, add soy grits and seasonings, and cook 5 minutes. A small amount of soy sauce or yeast paste seasoning may also be added. Serves 4.

⮜§ CREAM OF TOMATO SOUP

Add desired amount of medium soy grits or puffed grits to cream of tomato soup just before serving. Puffed soy grits can be used as croutons.

✒ CREAM OF PEA SOUP

Put 1 can green peas through a sieve or liquefy; add 1½ cups rich soy milk. Salt to taste. Serve hot with croutons. Serves 4.

✒ SOY CREAM OF TOMATO SOUP

1 can tomato juice
½ cup soy milk

Pour tomato juice in saucepan and heat. Heat milk in double boiler. Gradually add hot tomato juice to soy milk, stirring constantly. Serve at once—do not boil. Concentrated soups may be used in place of juice. Serves 4.

✒ DR. DEKLEINE'S VICTORY SOUP

7 tbs. food or brewer's yeast powder
½ lb. powdered skim milk
½ lb. soybean milk powder or toasted soy flour

Mix all together and store in covered jar. For soup, use ⅓ cup to each pint of liquid—stock, milk, bouillon, or canned soup. The yeast is rich in the B vitamins. The milk and flour are rich in protein and minerals.

✒ MINESTRONE SOUP

2 cups water
2 vegetable bouillon cubes
2 cups cooked lentils
½ tsp. M.S.G.
¼ tsp. cominos

¼ tsp. tarragon
¼ tsp. George Washington Golden Broth
 1 can (No. 2½) tomatoes (3¼ cups)
½ cup cabbage, shredded
 1 clove garlic
½ cup soy elbow macaroni (small size)
 1 can (No. 303) mixed vegetables and juice
 1 tbs. smoke flavor
Salt to taste

Bring water to boil in 3-quart saucepan. Add and dissolve
bouillon cubes. Add lentils; cover, and bring to a boil.
Add M.S.G., herbs, George Washington seasoning, tomatoes, and cabbage. Mix thoroughly. Insert wooden pick
into garlic clove and add to soup. Simmer for 25 minutes.
Add macaroni, vegetables and juice, and smoke flavor.
Cook until macaroni is tender—about 10 minutes. Remove garlic clove, add salt and adjust seasoning, and serve.
Makes 2 qts.

✑ PORTUGUESE RED BEAN SOUP

 2 cups uncooked red beans
 1 small onion, sliced
 1 clove garlic, cut fine (optional)
 1 large potato (scrub, but don't peel)
Salt to taste
 1 tsp. paprika
 1 tbs. oil
½ cup uncooked soy macaroni
 1 can (8-oz.) tomato sauce
 2 qts. water·
 1 small head cabbage, chopped
 2 tbs. lemon juice

Cook beans in plenty of water until done, or use 4 cups cooked beans. Add onion, garlic, potato, salt, paprika, oil, and macaroni. Add more water if necessary. Cook 15 minutes. Add tomato sauce, water (reduce to 1½ qts. if cooked beans are used), and cabbage, and cook 10 or 15 minutes more. Add lemon juice just before serving, and correct the salt. Makes 3½ to 4 qts.

This soup will freeze well for later use.

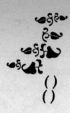

( )
( )

SALADS

The cook's ingenuity and imagination are the only limits to making a salad, and soybeans lend themselves to almost every combination. Green beans and whole canned or cooked beans can be used in vegetable and molded salads, soy sprouts can be used cooked or raw (see recipes in those sections), and roasted beans are good substitutes for nuts. Ground roasted soybeans make excellent toppings for fruit salads. Soy cheese can be used as cottage cheese (see cheese recipes), and diced soy roasts and loaves are excellent replacements for meat or fish in salads.

Salad Recipes

◄§ PLAIN SOY SALAD

  2 cups cooked soybeans
  1 cup chopped celery

Mix soybeans with chopped celery. Serve on lettuce with French or mayonnaise dressing. Serves 4.

✎§ SOY BEET SALAD

    2 cups cooked and well-drained beets, diced or shredded
    1 cup diced celery
    2 cups dry or green cooked soybeans

Mix well. Moisten with soy mayonnaise. Serve in large bowl, decorate with watercress, and add a dash of French dressing. Serves 6.

✎§ SOYBEAN VEGETABLE SALAD

    1 can or 2 cups cooked soybeans
    1 cup celery, chopped
    1 cup cooked carrots, diced or shoestring
    ½ cup cucumber, diced
    Watercress
    Tomato slices

Drain beans, add celery, carrots, cucumber, and a small amount of watercress. Mix well, moisten with French dressing or soy mayonnaise, and place in lettuce-lined salad dish. Decorate with sliced tomatoes. Serves 4 to 6.

✎§ SOY VEGETABLE PLATTER

    2 cups cooked soybeans
    1 cup celery, chopped
    1 cup cucumber, diced
    ½ cup radishes, sliced
    Asparagus tips

Tomato slices
Watercress
Ripe or green olives

Mix soybeans with celery, cucumber, and sliced radishes.
Moisten with French dressing and place in a mound in
the center of a large lettuce-lined platter. Surround edge
with asparagus tips and sliced tomatoes. Add sprays of watercress and ripe or green olives. Serves 4 to 5.

◆§ MOLDED SOY SALAD

1 pkg. lime- or lemon-flavored vegetable gelatin
1 cup mashed soybeans
1 cup diced cucumber or finely shredded cabbage
¼ cup minced watercress

Make vegetable gelatin according to recipe on package,
using ¼ cup less water. Then add beans, cucumber or
cabbage, and watercress. Chill until firm. Cut in slices and
serve on lettuce with French dressing. Serves 4.

◆§ SOY WALDORF SALAD

2 cups apple, chopped
2 cups celery, chopped
Soy mayonnaise
1 cup soy nuts (roasted soybeans), chopped or coarsely
ground
Mint leaves or watercress

Mix apple, celery, and soy nuts. Moisten with desired
amount of dressing. Serve on crisp lettuce; decorate with
mint leaves or sprigs of watercress. Serves 4 to 5.

⋖§ SOY FRUIT SALAD

    ½ cup raisins
    1 cup apple, chopped
    1 cup green or cooked soybeans
    ½ cup celery, chopped
    1 medium-sized avocado, diced
    Soy mayonnaise

Mix all together, chill, and serve on crisp lettuce. Serves 4.

⋖§ MOCK CHICKEN SALAD

    1 medium-sized can (2 cups) soy cheese, diced
    2 cups chopped celery
    1 cup diced cucumber
    3 cubed tomatoes
    Soy mayonnaise
    Tomato wedges
    Watercress
    Ripe olives

Remove soy cheese from can and dice. Mix all ingredients together; add desired seasoning and mayonnaise. Serve on crisp lettuce; decorate with wedges of tomato, watercress, and ripe olives. Serves 4 to 5.

⋖§ MOCK TUNA SALAD

    1 medium-sized can (2 cups) light-colored soy meat substitute
    1 can tiny peas, or 1 pkg. small frozen peas
    1 cup celery
    1 cup finely grated carrots

French dressing
4 tomatoes, cut in wedges
Avocado strips

Remove soy meat substitute from can and shred. Mix with rest of ingredients; add seasoning and French dressing. Serve in lettuce-lined salad bowl. Decorate with strips of avocado and tomato wedges. Avocado may be diced and added to salad. Serves 4 to 6.

◆§ SOY CHEESE SALAD AND SANDWICH SPREAD

2 cups soy cheese (fresh-steamed or canned), mashed
¼ cup parsley, chopped
2 tbs. mayonnaise
¼ cup celery, chopped
2 pimientos, chopped
¼ cup chopped olives

Mix thoroughly and serve cold. Use as sandwich filling or as a salad. Put in center of tomato cut in fourths and spread open or on tomato slices. Make sandwich of 2 tomato slices with this between, or use 2 pineapple slices with soy cheese salad between them. Serves 2 to 3.

◆§ POTATO SOY CHEESE SALAD

2 cups boiled potatoes, chopped
1 cup soy cheese
½ cup celery, chopped
1 large cucumber, diced
Soy mayonnaise

Mix potatoes, cheese, celery, and cucumber with mayonnaise. Serve on lettuce-lined salad platter and decorate with radish roses. Serves 4.

৺ STUFFED TOMATO SALAD

1 medium-sized can (2 cups) soy cheese
Soy mayonnaise
4 tomatoes, scooped out
2 tbs. celery, chopped
Watercress
French dressing

Mix soy cheese with mayonnaise and celery. Fill tomatoes with mixture. Serve on a bed of watercress with French dressing.

Salad Dressing Recipes

Soy oil may be used for any salad dressing. Follow favorite recipe, substituting soy for other oil. Dressings may also be made by thinning soy spreads.

৺ SOY CHEESE DRESSING

Fresh or canned soy cheese may be made into a dressing by mashing and thinning with tomato sauce. Add desired seasoning.

৺ TOASTED SOY BUTTER DRESSING

4 tbs. toasted soy butter
Tomato juice

Juice of ½ lemon
2 tbs. ripe olives, minced
2 tbs. celery, minced
4 or 5 tbs. watercress, minced
Seasonings as desired

Thin soy butter with tomato juice. Beat until smooth.
Add lemon juice, olives, celery, watercress, and any seasonings desired. Serve on head lettuce. Makes about 1 cup
dressing.

✠ BOILED SALAD DRESSING

2 eggs
4 tbs. soy flour
4 tbs. brown sugar
1 tsp. salt
3 tsp. powdered vegetable broth
⅔ cup soy milk
4 tbs. oil
½ cup lemon juice

Beat eggs slightly in top of double boiler. Add combined
dry ingredients; mix well. Add soy milk. Cook over rapidly
boiling water until mixture thickens (about 10 minutes),
stirring constantly. Remove from heat. Add oil and lemon
juice gradually. Chill. Makes about 1 pt. dressing.

✠ LEMON FRENCH DRESSING

⅓ cup soy oil
1 tsp. honey
¼ tsp. paprika
⅓ cup lemon juice (about 2 lemons)
½ tsp. salt

Combine all ingredients in small jar with screw top. Shake until blended. Chill until serving time.

◆§ HONEY FRENCH DRESSING

  1 cup olive or soy oil
  1 cup tomato sauce
  1 cup lemon juice
  1 cup honey
  1 tsp. salt
  Dash paprika

Blend in liquefier or mixer or pour into large jar and shake well. Can be used on either fruit or vegetable salads.

◆§ HAWAIIAN FRENCH DRESSING

  ¼ cup pineapple juice
  2 tbs. lemon juice
  ½ cup soy oil
  ½ tsp. salt
  ½ tsp. paprika

Combine all ingredients; chill. Shake or beat thoroughly before serving. If more sweetening is desired, add 1 tsp. raw sugar or honey. This dressing is excellent for fruit salads.

◆§ BANANA FRENCH DRESSING

Add 2 thoroughly mashed ripe bananas to the above dressing.

⋐§ SOY MAYONNAISE 1

Soy mayonnaise may be used for salads and in any way regular salad dressing is used. It may be diluted and used as a dip for cutlets or patties before browning, and it is a nutritious binder for timbales or croquettes.

1 cup water
½ cup all-purpose soy milk powder
½ tsp. salt
½ tsp. M.S.G.
½ tsp. paprika
1 cup oil
Juice of 1 lemon (about ¼ cup)

Make in a liquefier, putting in water, soy milk powder, salt, and seasoning; then add oil gradually until mixture thickens. Remove from liquefier and add lemon juice. May also be seasoned with onion or garlic.

When using an electric mixer or bowl and egg beater instead of liquefier, use ½ cup water instead of 1 cup and increase oil to 1¼ cups. Beat the water, soy milk, and seasonings, and add the oil slowly while beating. Then add lemon juice.

Cut calories by diluting with tomato juice, buttermilk, or yogurt.

⋐§ SOY MAYONNAISE 2

2 tbs. soy flour
3 to 4 tbs. water
1 cup vegetable oil
Salt
Seasoning
Juice of ½ lemon

Mix flour and water, and cook until thick and smooth. Gradually beat in oil. When thick, add salt, desired seasoning, and the lemon juice. In this, the soy flour acts as egg with the oil. It should be made in small quantities and used within a few days as it does not keep well.

✑ SANDWICH RELISH

    2 cups soy mayonnaise
    ¼ cup dill pickle, chopped
    ¼ cup celery, chopped
    2 green onions, chopped
    2 tsp. turmeric (dissolve in small amount of water before
       adding)
    1 tbs. honey
    1 tbs. pimiento, chopped
    ½ tsp. Italian herbs
    ¼ tsp. sweet basil
    1 tbs. parsley, chopped
    1 tbs. yeast paste

Mix thoroughly and use as a spread on vegetable burger and any other sandwiches.

✑ TROPICAL DRESSING

    1 cup soy mayonnaise
    ½ cup pineapple, crushed
    1 banana, mashed
    ¼ cup fresh coconut, grated

Mix thoroughly. Use on any kind of fruit salad.

◌ఏ PIQUANT DRESSING

1 cup soy mayonnaise
1 tbs. pimiento, chopped
½ cup cucumber, shredded
1 tbs. lemon juice

Mix and chill. Use as accompanying sauce for protein dishes, salads, and cooked vegetables.

◌ఏ SPREAD DELUXE

1 cup soy mayonnaise
1 tsp. dehydrated onions
1 tsp. yeast paste
1 tsp. dehydrated parsley

Mix thoroughly and allow to stand at least an hour. Use as a spread on toast, crackers, or rye crisps, or as a dunk for stick vegetables—celery, carrots, raw broccoli, etc. This is delicious on green salads.

◌ఏ ZIPPY DRESSING

1 cup soy mayonnaise
¼ cup tomato juice
1 tbs. chopped parsley
1 tbs. chives or green onions
Garlic salt to taste
Celery salt to taste

Mix thoroughly. Use on vegetable salads, cooked or raw.

⋐ TARTAR SAUCE

- 1 cup soy mayonnaise
- 2 tbs. lemon juice
- ½ cup soy cheese
- Salt to taste
- Paprika to taste
- ½ tsp. capers
- 1 tbs. onion, chopped
- 1 tbs. dill pickle, chopped
- 1 tbs. pimiento, chopped
- 1 tbs. parsley, chopped
- 1 tbs. green pepper, chopped

Mix all ingredients together lightly.

SOY SPREADS
AND SOY BUTTER

Soy spreads have been on the market for many years, but until the last few years their sale was limited to specialty food stores; today they are more widely purchasable. Some spreads contain only soybeans, and others are a combination of beans, nuts, and grains. Some are highly seasoned to resemble bologna, and others are very mild in flavor. Often minced ripe olives or pimiento are added. A few spreads are made from soy cheese, but most of them contain bean pulp or soy grits. Such spreads are easily made at home and can be seasoned to suit the family taste. Mashed soybeans can also be used as sandwich spreads.

Soy Spread Recipes

❧ SOY CHEESE SPREAD

Canned soy cheese may be used as a sandwich spread plain or mixed with peanut butter, minced olives, or chopped celery.

❧ STUFFED CELERY

Fill strips of celery with canned or homemade soy spread. Chill before serving.

❧ SOY OLIVE SPREAD

1 cup cooked soy grits
1 tbs. powdered vegetable broth
¼ tsp. salt
2 tsp. soy sauce or yeast extract
½ cup minced ripe olives
Tomato juice or sauce to moisten

Cook grits in 2 cups of boiling water until dry. Add seasoning. Celery and onion salt may be substituted for vegetable broth. Add ripe olives and just enough tomato juice or sauce to moisten.

This spread will keep for several days in the refrigerator. It may also be made into patties or meat balls and browned in oil. They may be served hot or used as cold cuts in sandwiches.

⌔§ EGG AND SOY SPREAD

2 hard-cooked egg yolks
½ cup canned soy cheese
Salt, lemon juice, mayonnaise to taste

Rub egg yolks through sieve, mix with soy cheese, and
season as desired. This is very good as a sandwich filling
with lettuce.

⌔§ SOY VEGETABLE SPREAD

1 cup canned or cooked soybeans, mashed
1 tsp. powdered vegetable broth
½ cup celery, minced
2 tbs. parsley, minced

Mash soybeans; add powdered vegetable broth and minced
vegetables. Moisten with desired amount of mayonnaise
and use as sandwich spread.

⌔§ SOY AVOCADO SPREAD

Mix equal parts of soy spread with mashed avocado.
Usually extra seasoning is not necessary. Minced olives,
pimiento, or veegtables may be added, and/or soy mayonnaise.

⌔§ SOY AVOCADO NUT SPREAD

1 medium-sized avocado, mashed
½ cup soybeans, mashed
½ cup nut meal (finely ground soy nuts)
2 tbs. or more lemon juice
Seasoning to taste

Peel and mash avocado; add mashed cooked beans and nut meal. Mix well. Add lemon juice and seasoning to taste.

⊷§ COOKED SOY SPREAD

  ¾ cup all-purpose soy milk powder
  1 tbs. cornstarch
  ¾ tbs. salt
  ¾ cup water
  1 tbs. lemon juice
  2 cups corn oil
  Few drops yellow vegetable coloring

Mix soy milk powder, cornstarch, and salt; then add water and lemon juice. Cook in top of double boiler until thick (5 or 6 minutes), stirring frequently. Remove from double boiler to bowl, and while still hot, add oil, ¼ cup at a time, beating thoroughly with egg beater or electric mixer after each addition of oil. Repeat until all oil is used and product is very thick. Add coloring and mix. Place in refrigerator. Will keep for a week or 10 days. Use as spread on bread or toast, or as sauce for baked potato or vegetables.

⊷§ YEASTY SPREAD 1

  Food yeast
  1 cup soy mayonnaise
  Sprinkle of onion and garlic salt

Mix enough food yeast with mayonnaise to make a thick spread. This low-fat mixture is good on toast, crackers, bread, or baked potato.

⊷ YEASTY SPREAD 2

1 cup tomato juice or mixed vegetable juice
¼ tsp. powdered celery seed
2 tbs. soy sauce
2 tbs. toasted soy flour or powder
¼ tsp. powdered onion (optional)
Enough food yeast to thicken

Bring first five ingredients to rolling boil. Allow to cool, and then mix with yeast to make good spreading consistency. Use in place of margarine or butter on toast, crackers, bread, or baked potato.

Soy Butter Recipes

A butter resembling peanut butter can be made from finely ground soybeans or soy flour. Do not use raw beans or flour for this because raw soybeans are indigestible unless properly cooked or processed. Soy butter may be used like any nut butter, for spreads, and in cooking or baking. The flavor is improved by the addition of a small amount of honey. Thinned soy butter may be used as a salad dressing.

Soy butter contains from 40 to 50 percent protein, and since oil is added, it is very rich in fat. It is a rich, concentrated food, and therefore should be used sparingly.

⊷ ROASTED SOY BUTTER

Roasted soy butter is made from the roasted beans that have been ground into a fine flour. Oil is gradually beaten in until the mixture is the consistency of peanut butter.

The darkness of the color depends on how well the beans are roasted. Salt may be added if needed.

Browned soy flour may be used if desired. To brown soy flour, place in shallow pan and brown in slow oven. Stir for even browning.

✍ CRUNCHY SOY BUTTER

Make roasted soy butter in the usual manner, adding a little more oil. When well blended, add the desired amount of finely ground roasted soybeans. Do not add salt, for the roasted beans are salty.

✍ SOY BUTTER AND APPLES

Soy butter goes very well with raw fruit or raw vegetables. Those who want to avoid eating bread may enjoy an apple sandwich. Slice a large unpeeled apple into thin slices. Spread each slice with a small amount of soy butter. Two slices may be placed together with a soy butter filling.

✍ SOY BUTTER AND CELERY

Stuff small celery stalks with roasted soy butter. Serve with salads.

✍ SOY BUTTER AND HONEY

8 tbs. roasted soy butter
4 tbs. honey

Mix well. Use like peanut butter.

✎ SOY BUTTER AND OLIVES

½ cup roasted soy butter
3 tbs. ripe olives, minced

Mix well and use as sandwich spread.

✎ SOY BUTTER AND AVOCADO

Mash one ripe avocado; add desired amount of roasted soy butter. Mix well. Use as spread on whole wheat bread or crackers or with raw fruit or vegetables.

✎ SOY BUTTER SPREAD

4 tbs. soy butter
3 tbs. minced dill pickles
3 tbs. lemon juice
1 tbs. soy mayonnaise or cooked soy spread

Mix well. Prepared soy spread may be used instead of soy butter.

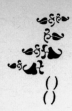

SOY MILK

Soy milk is a white or creamy emulsion resembling cow's milk in both appearance and consistency. It may be used in any recipe calling for dairy milk, and in the same proportions. This excellent nutritious liquid has proved a valuable food in allergy and special diets, and as already pointed out, it has been used in the Orient for centuries. In addition to the recipes below, recipes in the sections on soups, salad dressings, sauces and gravies, and desserts show delicious ways to use soy milk.

Like dairy milk, the soy liquid will sour; if putrefaction does not set in, the curd may be boiled and strained like cottage cheese, making soy cheese, which will be discussed in the next chapter.

Soy milk is now sold in cans as condensed milk; the canned milk is fortified with minerals, fat, and carbohydrate to equal cow's or mother's milk in food value.

◄§ SOY POWDER

Soy powder for milk is ready to use, and serves as a base for many a delicious beverage. It can be added to any liquid—water, milk, juice, or soup. For plain soy milk, 4 tablespoons of powder should be added to each cup of water and stirred until well blended. The powder may be sweetened with dextrose, as with powdered banana and coconut, which also add flavor. The made-up liquid may be sweetened with a small amount of honey, molasses, or sugar.

Rich Soy Milk Rich soy milk is made by using 1½ to 2 times the amount of powder called for in the directions on the can or package.

◄§ SOY MALT

Soy malt in various flavors has been on the market for several years and has gained steadily in popularity. Soy malts are made from soy powder or low-fat soy flour with malt, sweetening, and flavoring added. The most popular flavors are vanilla and chocolate; coconut, banana, and almond are also available. Soy malts are sold under various trade names, and a soy milk powder with malt flavor is also available.

How to Make Soy Milk

◄§ SOY MILK FROM DRY BEANS

Oriental Method Several methods are used in the Orient for making soy milk. The following is perhaps the simplest.

Soak dry soybeans in water for 12 hours at room temperature, changing the water frequently. Many prefer to soak the beans at least 24 hours. Grind the beans to a fine paste, in a food chopper with a fine knife or, preferably, in a stone mill, adding water to the mass during the grinding process in the amount of 3 times the bulk of the beans. Boil this mass to foaming for 1 hour, and then strain through cheesecloth.

Bag Method Wash the dry beans and soak them overnight. In the morning, drain them and remove the loose skins. Grind the beans very fine, and then place them in a cheesecloth bag. Put the bag in a large bowl of lukewarm water, using 3 quarts of water to each pound of dry beans. Work thoroughly with the hands for 5 to 10 minutes. Wring the bag of pulp until it is dry. Boil the milk over a low flame for 30 minutes, stirring constantly to prevent scorching. Add salt and a small amount of honey or sweetening. This milk will keep several days in the refrigerator.

Quick Method This method is less work and gives a good soy milk. Soak 1 cup of dry beans overnight. Drain them and run them through a food chopper, using a fine knife. Add 6 cups of water to the ground beans and bring the mixture to a boil. Simmer for 15 minutes; strain through a fine sieve or cheesecloth. Flavor the milk as desired. A liquefier may be used for grinding the beans. If a double boiler is used for cooking the liquid or ground beans, double the cooking time (to 30 minutes).

Madison College Method This method of preparing soy milk calls for the following ingredients:

1½ lbs. dry soybeans
1 cup soy, corn, or cottonseed oil
3 tsp. salt
1¾ cups dextrose

Cover the soybeans well with water and soak them overnight. Grind them fine in a small grinder, pouring a small stream of water into the grinder continuously to prevent clogging. Add water until the volume of the ground mixture is 1 gallon. Heat this in a large pan, preferably enamel, with continuous stirring until it is too hot for the finger to remain immersed in it. Place the mixture in cheesecloth or a flour sack, using the hands to squeeze out the milk. Boil the milk in an enamel pan for 45 minutes, stirring constantly. Take 2 cups of hot milk and pour them into a liquefier. Add the oil, and whiz for 5 minutes. An electric mixer or egg beater can be used in place of the liquefier, but the results are not so satisfactory, and a longer time is required to obtain a good emulsion. Pour the oil and milk into the remainder of the milk and stir. Add the salt and dextrose. If dextrose is not available, use corn syrup, honey, or some other form of sugar, and sweeten to taste. Boil for 15 minutes. Add enough water to make 5 quarts, and cool the mixture quickly. Keep it in glass jars or bottles, tightly covered and well refrigerated.

☙ SOY MILK FROM SOY FLOUR

Mix 4 cups of water and 1 cup of flour gradually so that the mixture does not become lumpy. Let it stand 2 hours; cook it in a double boiler for 40 minutes, and then strain it through a sieve or cheesecloth. Flavor the milk with a small amount of honey and salt. Add more water if necessary for desired consistency.

Soy Yogurt

Soy yogurt is both nutritious and tasty; it may be used as a beverage like buttermilk, or over fruit and berries as are dairy yogurt and sour cream. Any recipe calling for sour cream can be made with soy yogurt instead, and the yogurt alone may be sweetened with honey and used as a dessert.

To make soy yogurt, use ¼ cup yogurt culture to each quart of liquid soy milk. A number of commercial yogurt cultures are available, among them Soyadophilus and Theradophilus, which may be purchased at specialty food stores or ordered from Therapy Ltd., North Hollywood, California.

Warm the liquid soy milk and yogurt culture to blood temperature and put it in a sterile jar. Keep the jar in a warm place for 2 or 3 hours, or until the mixture has reached the desired thickness—the pilot light on the stove works very well.

When making a new batch, use 1 cup of this as a starter and proceed as above.

Soy Milk Recipes

◅§ LIQUEFIED SOY MILK DRINKS

Delicious soy milk drinks can be made in a liquefier or in a malted milk mixer. Add 1 to 2 tbs. soy powder or soy milk to juice or desired liquid.

Soy milk may be liquefied with a few nuts—almonds, cashews, sunflower seeds, sesame seeds, peanuts, pecans— to give a variety in the flavor. It may also be liquefied with dates, bananas, berries, or any other fruit or fruit juice.

✑§ CASHEW CREAM

    1 cup rich soy milk
    1 tsp. honey, or 1 or 2 dates
  ½ cup cashews
    Pinch of salt

Liquefy all together for 2 or 3 minutes. Delicious over cereal. Thin down if used for drinking.

✑§ GREEN DRINK

    1 cup pineapple juice
    1 tbs. soy milk powder
  ¼ cup or less fresh alfalfa
  ¼ cup or less parsley

Liquefy pineapple juice and soy milk powder. Add alfalfa and parsley. Whiz a minute, strain, and serve cold.

    Powdered alfalfa may be substituted for fresh, or it may be omitted entirely.

✑§ MELON SEED DRINK

    Seeds from 1 melon
    1 cup water
    1 to 2 tbs. powdered soy milk
    Honey or molasses

Liquefy melon seeds with water for 3 or 4 minutes. Strain through fine sieve and return to liquefier. Add powdered soy milk and whiz until thoroughly blended. Honey or molasses may be added if not sweet enough.

☙ COCONUT MILK

1 cup warm water
Sprinkle of salt
1 cup unsweetened grated coconut
Honey to taste

Liquefy for 3 minutes. Strain.

☙ CHRISTMAS NOG

1 cup soy milk
1 tbs. soy milk powder
¼ tsp. vanilla
1 tbs. corn oil
1 tsp. lecithin (liquid or granules)
Few drops almond flavoring

Liquefy all ingredients until light and fluffy. Serve cold or hot (but do not boil). For large amounts, simply multiply the ingredients. Soy milk used may be fresh, canned, or made from powder (either malt or all-purpose).

As variations, garnish with grated lemon or orange rind, a sprinkle of anise seed or oil of anise, or powdered cardamon or coriander seed; or add 1 tsp. carob powder. Also, the soy milk may be liquified with a few nuts or any fruit or fruit juice.

⋖ஃ FROZEN SOY DRINKS

Whiz in liquefier any frozen fruit with soy milk for a delicious drink. You can freeze in your ice tray any fruit, such as canned peaches and apricots; use this with the soy milk.

⋖ஃ MIXED SOY DRINKS

Fruit and vegetable juices may be mixed with soy milk or powder to make delicious drinks. These do not require use of a liquifier.

⋖ஃ CARROT SOY MILK

Mix equal parts soy milk and fresh carrot juice. If using soy powder, add 1 or 2 tbs. powder to each glass of carrot juice, and mix well.

⋖ஃ HIGH-PROTEIN BEVERAGE

   1 cup liquid soy milk
   1 level tbs. food or brewer's yeast
  ¼ cup toasted soy flour
   Flavoring

Mix thoroughly and serve. Flavoring may be one of a number—orange, lemon, vanilla, molasses, boysenberry punch.

⋖ஃ SOY AND FIG BEVERAGE

  ¾ cup soy milk
  ¼ cup fig juice

Mix thoroughly. Serve cold or hot (but do not boil).

❧ SOY AND COCONUT BEVERAGE

1 cup coconut milk
2 level tbs. soy milk powder

Mix thoroughly. Serve cold or hot (but do not boil).

❧ 'LASSES SHAKE

1 tsp. to 1 tbs. molasses
1 glass soy milk

Shake well. Serve cold or hot (but do not boil).

Soy Malt Recipes

Soy malt beverages, made with commercial soy malt, can be made in a wide variety of flavors. In addition, flavored soy malt may be used in custards, desserts, ice creams, sauces, candies, cakes, and cookies. It is excellent added to eggnog.

❧ HOT SOY MALT

1 tbs. soy malt
Hot water
Hot milk
Honey

Place soy malt in a cup. Add enough hot water to make a smooth paste. Fill cup with hot milk, or use more hot water, adding cream as desired. A small amount of honey may be added if not sweet enough.

✍§ CAROB MALT BEVERAGE

 1 cup malt soy milk, made from powder
 1 tsp. carob powder
 ½ tsp. vanilla
 Pinch of salt

Mix malt soy milk powder according to directions. Add carob powder, vanilla, and salt to the cup. Mix thoroughly. Serve either hot or cold.

✍§ SOY SHAKE

 2 tbs. soy malt powder
 1 cup of water
 1 cup milk (soy or dairy)
 ½ cup cracked ice
 1 banana, sliced
 1 or 2 tbs. honey

Pour water into liquefier or mixer. Add soy malt powder and blend well. Add milk, ice, and banana. Whip until thoroughly blended. Sweeten as desired.

As variations, strawberries, peaches, or other fruit may be used in place of banana.

TOFU OR
SOY CHEESE

Tofu, "the meat without a bone," is perhaps the most unusual and to many the most fascinating of all soybean foods. By all means, try it in a Chinese restaurant. Properly prepared, it is delicious.

Fresh Tofu The fresh cheese may be made at home, or it may be purchased in an Oriental food store, where it is made fresh daily. It is a white, tasteless cake that needs pepping up; a pinch of salt or celery salt, tomato juice, a little onion juice, and soy sauce are tasty basic seasonings. Properly prepared, tofu may be used as meat, fish, cheese, sandwich spread, or dessert. Mashed and seasoned, it resembles cottage cheese; sliced and cooked, it becomes a meat or fish entree; and sweetened, it is a light, delicate dessert. If used in salads, it should be steamed or pressure-cooked first.

Fresh tofu is very fragile and is kept under water as it

spoils quickly. It will keep for several days in water in the refrigerator.

Canned Tofu A few commercial companies can soy cheese under various other names—soy food, vegetable cheese, soy curd, or their own trade names. When canned, it is in fine curds resembling farmer-style cottage cheese. It may be plain or seasoned with soy sauce or pimiento. Often it is rather moist. Canned soy cheese may be used like cottage cheese for spreads and salads, or sliced and heated and served as a meat replacement.

Frozen Tofu Tofu may be sliced and frozen, either in water or out of it. It should be wrapped thoroughly. A brick or cake of soy cheese makes approximately 1 cup mashed. To defrost, the desired number of frozen bricks should be covered in tepid water and let stand for several hours or overnight; the water need not be kept tepid during the defrosting. When the brick is thawed, it should be removed from the water, pressed slightly with the hands to remove excess water, and used immediately.

How to Make Soy Cheese

✎§ SOY CHEESE FROM MILK

Soy cheese is made by allowing soy milk to sour and curdle. When it is made commercially, lactic, tartaric, or citric acid is used; but acid is not necessary when a small amount of cheese is made at home. Set the soy milk in a warm place to sour and thicken. When thick, cut it into chunks with a knife, place these in a pan, cover them with water, and bring to the boiling point. Strain through cheesecloth, wringing the curds as dry as possible. Season with salt and a small amount of soy sauce. The fresh cheese can be used like cottage cheese and can be stored in the refrigerator for several days.

✑§ SOY CHEESE FROM DRY SOYBEANS

For this method, you will need the following ingredients:

1 cup dry soybeans (yellow mammoth are good)
4 cups water
Juice of 2 lemons

Soak the beans overnight, drain the liquid off, and wash the beans thoroughly. Using ½ cup beans to 1 cup water, run them in a liquefier for 2 to 3 minutes. Strain the mixture through a fine sieve. Save both the liquid and pulp. When all the soaked beans have been liquefied, put all the pulp back in the liquefier with enough water to nearly cover. Liquefy this for about 2 minutes and strain it into the above liquid. This milk-like liquid is made into soy cheese as follows:

Bring the milk mixture to a rolling boil (a double boiler is good for this, as it sticks quite easily). Add the lemon juice, stirring only enough to mix thoroughly. Allow the mixture to stand in the heat until it is coagulated. This soy cheese may be used in any recipe calling for soy cheese or tofu.

This cheese may be used as a base for patties, loaves, or other entrées. If it is used in salads or other dishes where it will not be cooked, it should be boiled in water for 15 to 20 minutes before using.

The residue left when making soy cheese from the whole beans may be used in making bread and cookies, or in a loaf to be used as an entrée.

◄§ SOY CHEESE FROM FLOUR

This method calls for the following ingredients:

1 cup full-fat soy flour
3 cups water
Juice of 2 lemons

Place the water in a saucepan and bring it to a boil. Mix a cup of full-fat soy flour to a paste with cold water. Beat it with an egg beater 1 minute and add it to the boiling water in the saucepan. Let this cook about 5 minutes; then add the lemon juice, and set the mixture aside to cool. Strain the curds through a fine strainer or cheesecloth. This cheese can be used as a base for patties, loaves, and other entrées, or it may be pressure-cooked for 1 hour at 10 lbs. pressure and served in salads.

Soy Cheese Recipes

◄§ TOFU STEAK 1

1 cake fresh soy cheese
Salt
½ tsp. or more soy sauce or other meatlike sauce

Place cake of tofu on a rack in a small amount of water, or tie in cheesecloth in water, and cook for 20 minutes. Tofu varies as to firmness depending on method of preparation.

The soft cakes require careful handling. When cooking, it is always advisable to place the cake on a rack, for the flat surface against the pan has a tendency to burn.

When cooked, slice cake into ½″ to 1″ slices. Place in greased baking pan, sprinkle with salt, and top with soy or other meatlike sauce. The sauce will penetrate the tofu and give it a decided meatlike flavor. Dot each slice with margarine or oil and brown in hot oven or under broiler. Serve hot. Serves 2.

If there is no objection to fried food, slices may be seasoned with salt and soy sauce and fried in fat, or dipped in crumbs or flour and then fried. Serve with gravy or tomato sauce. Cooked tofu is tasty when cold and can be used as fried meat or eggs for sandwiches.

⊷ TOFU STEAK 2

1 can soy cheese (16 to 20 oz.)
Minced parsley

Open both ends of can. Remove soy cheese as cylinder. Slice in ½″ slices. Brown in oil or under broiler, and serve with minced parsley. Serves 4 to 5.

⊷ SOY SHEPHERD'S PIE

2 tbs. oil
1 large onion, diced
1½ cups water
1 tbs. yeast paste
¼ tsp. salt
1 tsp. powdered vegetable broth
2 tbs. whole wheat flour
2 cups soy cheese (canned or fresh)

1 tbs. minced parsley
Mashed potatoes

Brown diced onion in oil; add water, yeast paste, and seasoning. Thicken with flour rubbed smooth with a little cold water. Add soy cheese and minced parsley. Place in greased casserole and top with mashed potatoes. Bake until light brown. Serves 4.

⋑ TOFU LOAF

  2 tbs. oil
  2 tbs. onion, chopped
  ⅓ cup green pepper, chopped
  1 cup tofu, mashed
  1 cup soy milk
  ½ cup breadcrumbs
  1 cup English walnuts, chopped
  ¼ cup dry instant mashed potatoes

Place oil, onion, and green pepper in saucepan and simmer until soft but not brown. Mash tofu with fork and add milk to it; mix well. Add crumbs and nuts, then onion and pepper; add dry instant mashed potatoes last, and mix well. Season to taste. Place in oiled loaf pan and bake in moderate oven for about 1 hour, or until nicely browned on top. Garnish with parsley and serve with any desired sauce. Serves 4 to 6.

⋑ TOFU OATMEAL LOAF

  2 tbs. oil
  3 tbs. onion, diced
  2 cups tofu, mashed

1 cup oatmeal or other cereal, cooked
¼ tsp. lemon juice
1 cup walnuts, chopped fine
¼ cup cereal crumbs
¼ cup dry instant mashed potatoes

Place oil and onion in a saucepan and simmer until onion is soft but not brown. Mash tofu with fork and combine with oatmeal. Add lemon juice, walnuts, and crumbs. Add onion and oil mixture and dry instant mashed potatoes. Mix thoroughly and adjust seasoning. Place in oiled loaf pan. Bake in moderate oven for about 1 hour, or until well done and nicely browned on top. Garnish with parsley and serve with any desired sauce. Serves 4 to 6.

⋖§ TOFU CASSEROLE

2 tbs. oil
1 cup celery, chopped fine
½ tsp. onion, minced
2 tbs. parsley, minced
1 cup tofu, mashed
½ cup tomato soup
½ cup walnuts, chopped fine
2 tbs. dry breadcrumbs
¼ cup stuffed olives, sliced
1 tbs. dry instant mashed potatoes
½ tsp. lemon juice
¼ tsp, thyme, powdered

Place oil, celery, onion, and parsley in saucepan and simmer until soft but not brown. Mash tofu with fork and mix with canned tomato soup. Add nuts, crumbs, and sliced olives. Now add oil and vegetable mixture, and then dry instant mashed potatoes, lemon juice, and thyme. Adjust salt to taste. Mix thoroughly and place in oiled casserole. Bake in moderate oven about 45 minutes, or until nicely done and brown on top. Garnish with parsley and serve with any desired sauce. Tomato sauce is very good with this. Serves 4 to 6.

RICE SOY CHEESE CASSEROLE

> 2 cups brown rice, cooked
> Salt
> Powdered vegetable broth
> Canned soy cheese
> Milk (soy or dairy)
> Breadcrumbs

Season rice with salt and powdered vegetable broth. Place a layer of rice in a casserole, cover with a layer of soy cheese, and top with more rice. Fill casserole and add enough milk to almost cover. Sprinkle with breadcrumbs. Cover and bake 1 hour in moderate oven.

SOY CHEESE CUTLETS

Cut cake of fresh tofu in half lengthwise, then crosswise into ½-inch slices. Dip in beaten egg seasoned with celery salt. Dip in crumbs and fry in a small amount of oil until brown. Slices may be placed in well-oiled pan and baked until slightly brown. Serve with tomato or mushroom sauce.

✍ SOY CHEESE SCALLOPS

1½ lbs. soy cheese
2 eggs, scrambled
1 tsp. yeast extract
¼ tsp. salt
3 tbs. soy mayonnaise
2 eggs, raw
¼ cup onion, grated
¼ tsp. smoked flavoring
½ tsp, M.S.G.
2 tsp. soy sauce
Cereal flakes to thicken

Steam tofu 20 minutes; drain and cool. Mix all ingredients to right consistency to roll into balls. Roll in cereal flakes and fry in deep fat. May also be made into patties and browned on top of stove or in hot oven, or formed into loaf and baked. Serve with tartar sauce.

✍ SOY CHEESE FRITTERS FOR TWO

These are delicious and make a very inexpensive entrée.

2 eggs
1 cup soy cheese
1 tsp. soy sauce

Beat egg well. Add soy cheese and mix until well blended. Add soy sauce. Bake as pancakes in oil. Brown on one side and then turn. They will be tender and yet will not break. Serve hot with tart jelly.

✑ SOY CHEESE CROQUETTES 1

 1 egg, raw
 1 cup canned soy cheese
 2 tbs. oil
 2 hard-cooked eggs rubbed through sieve
 ½ tsp. yeast paste
 Salt, sage, and grated onion to taste
 Cracker crumbs or corn meal
 Minced parsley and tomato slices

Beat raw egg well, add rest of ingredients, mix, and shape into croquettes. Roll in cracker crumbs or corn meal, place in greased pan, and bake in moderate oven 20 minutes. Serve with minced parsley and sliced tomatoes. Croquettes may be made with fresh cheese and may be fried in oil if so desired. Serves 3.

✑ SOY CHEESE CROQUETTES 2

 2 cups soy cheese
 1 tbs. oil
 ½ tsp. salt
 2 green onions, chopped fine
 2 cups brown rice, cooked
 ¼ cup chopped parsley
 1 tsp. M.S.G.
 Pinch of sage

Mix all ingredients thoroughly and roll into small balls; then roll in crushed cereal flakes. Bake about ½ hour in a quick oven. Serve with mushroom sauce or tartar sauce. Serves 4 to 5.

❧ SOY CHEESE CROQUETTES 3

    ¾ cup all-purpose white flour
    6 tbs. oil
    1½ cups milk (dairy or soy)
    1 tsp. M.S.G.
    ⅛ tsp. paprika
    ¼ tsp. salt
    1 tsp. chopped parsley
    2 cups soy cheese, cubed
    1 cup whole wheat breadcrumbs

Make white sauce from flour, oil, and milk. Cook until thick, like dough or paste. Add all ingredients except breadcrumbs. Chill. Shape into croquettes and dip in egg and crumbs. Keep in refrigerator until time to bake. Bake in hot oven 5 to 8 minutes, just before serving. Serves 6 to 8.

❧ SOY CHEESE PATTIES 1

    2 tbs. olive oil
    2 tbs. onion, minced
    2 tbs. celery, chopped
    1 cup brown rice, cooked
    1 cup soy cheese
    1 cup green split peas, cooked soft
    ½ cup breadcrumbs
    1 tbs. soy sauce, or 1 tsp. yeast extract
    ⅔ tsp. salt

Sauté minced onion and chopped celery until lightly browned. Combine with all other ingredients. Form into patties; roll in crumbs. Place on oiled cookie sheet and turn so that both sides are oiled. Bake in moderate oven

20 to 25 minutes or until well browned. Serve plain or with a parsley white sauce or tartar sauce. Serves 6.

∙§ SOY CHEESE PATTIES 2

2 tbs. minced green onions
2 tbs. oil
1 cup tofu, mashed
¼ cup soy milk
¼ cup breadcrumbs
2 tbs. walnuts, chopped
3 tbs. dry instant mashed potatoes
¼ tsp. lemon juice

Place oil and onions in saucepan and simmer until onions are soft but not brown. Mash tofu with fork. Add soy milk to tofu; then add breadcrumbs and nuts and mix well. Add onion oil mixture. Add dry instant mashed potatoes and lemon juice. Mix thoroughly. Adjust seasoning. Oil hands slightly and form mixture into patties. Roll in very fine cereal flakes or crumbs and place on oiled sheet. Bake in moderate oven about ½ hour or until nicely browned. Makes 4 patties.

∙§ TOFU WITH MUSHROOM SAUCE

2 cups tofu, cubed
4 tbs. oil
1 bunch green onions, sliced thin
2 stalks celery, cut fine
1 small can mushrooms, sliced
1 tbs. soy sauce
3 tbs. flour
1 cup cold water

Put tofu in flat baking dish. Cover with sauce made as follows. Sauté in oil green onions, and celery until tender. Add mushrooms, soy sauce, flour, and water. Pour this sauce over tofu and let stand 1 or 2 hours until well blended. Reheat mixture in moderate oven 15 to 20 minutes, and serve. Serves 4.

◆§ TOFU WITH TOMATO SAUCE

    2 cups tofu, cubed
    2 tbs. oil
    2 tbs. onion, minced
    2 tbs. celery, minced
    2 tbs. bell pepper, minced
    1 can tomato soup or equivalent tomato sauce

Brown vegetables in oil and add tomato soup, diluted slightly. Put tofu in a casserole and pour sauce over it. Bake in moderate oven 30 minutes. Serve at once. Serves 4.

◆§ SOY CHEESE STUFFED PEPPER

Fill green pepper shells with canned soy cheese to which a few chopped ripe olives and a small amount of diced celery have been added. Brush lightly with oil and bake ¾ hour in moderate oven. Serve with tomato sauce.

◆§ SOY CHEESE STUFFED POTATO

Cut baked potatoes in half. Remove center and mash. Add ⅓ the amount of canned soy cheese, a little vegetable butter, powdered vegetable broth, and salt. Moisten with rich soy milk. Pack into shell and bake until brown on top.

⊷ SCALLOPED SOY CHEESE AND ONIONS

Place a layer of diced onions in a buttered casserole; cover with a layer of canned soy cheese and a few breadcrumbs. Alternate onions and cheese until casserole is full. Add a small amount of cream or soy milk, and top with bread-crumbs. Cover and bake in a moderate oven until done. This is delicious seasoned with soy sauce.

⊷ TOFU AND BEAN SPROUTS

1 cup tofu, cut in ½" cubes
1 cup mushrooms, chopped
¼ tsp. meatlike vegetable seasoning
1 tsp. vegetable chicken flavoring, or 1 tsp. M.S.G.
2 tbs. oil
1 cup celery, sliced
¾ cup broth (from cooking celery)
1 cup bean sprouts
3 tsp. cornstarch
2 tbs. soy sauce

Place tofu, mushrooms, vegetable seasoning, and oil in saucepan and simmer. Cut celery into rather large diagonal slices; parboil in ¾ cup water for 1 minute, and then add sprouts and continue to parboil about 2 minutes longer. Drain and use this liquid for vegetable broth. Add water if necessary to make right amount. Thicken broth with cornstarch, which has been dissolved in 1 tbs. cold water. Cook mixture until starch is thoroughly done, stirring constantly. Add soy sauce to thickened broth, and then mix all ingredients lightly while still hot. Serve at once.

❧ TOFU CHOP SUEY

      3 cups tofu, diced
      4 tbs. oil
  1½ cups onion, shredded
  1½ cups celery, chopped
      3 tbs. soy sauce
      1 cup water
      2 tbs. soy flour
      3 tbs. corn starch
  1½ cup bean sprouts

Brown tofu in oil. Add partly cooked onions, celery, soy
sauce, and water. Cook 5 minutes. Mix soy flour and cornstarch with a small amount of the liquid and add to mixture. Cook a few minutes longer. Add bean sprouts, cover,
and cook 5 minutes. Serve with brown rice. Serves 5 generously.

❧ ISLAND SUKIYAKI

      1 tbs. oil
      1 cup dry onion, halved and sliced
      2 cups gluten cutlets, sliced thin (about 1″ × 2″)
      3 heaping tsp. brown sugar
  ¼ cup soy sauce
      1 cup bamboo shoots, sliced
  ½ cup mushrooms, sliced
      1 cup green onions, cut in 1½″ lengths
      2 cups watercress, cut in 3″ lengths
  ½ bunch long rice, cut in 3″ lengths, washed and soaked
          in hot water for ½ hour
  ½ block tofu, cubed, or 1 cup canned soy cheese
  ¼ tsp. M.S.G.

Pour oil into skillet and heat. Add a few slices dry onion, stirring often over low heat to prevent burning. Add gluten cutlets and stir, browning slightly. Add sugar and soy sauce. Let mixture come to a boil *without* stirring. Add bamboo shoots, rest of dry onion, and mushrooms, and add greens last so as not to overcook them. Add long rice; when about cooked (transparent), add tofu and M.S.G. Serves 6 to 8.

As variations, more soy sauce and sugar may be used according to individual taste; and other ingredients, like green peppers, bean sprouts, tomatoes, chrysanthemum petals, turnips, and carrots, may be used.

◆§ FRESH SCRAMBLED TOFU

2 cups tofu, cut in ¾" cubes
Herb seasoning
Salt
M.S.G.

Oil fryer or bake pan. Put in tofu. Sprinkle with herb seasoning, salt, and a little M.S.G. If using fryer, cover and simmer over low fire until flavor has gone through—10 to 15 minutes; if in bake pan, place in moderate oven 20 to 30 minutes. A little tumeric or vegetable chicken flavoring may be added. Serves 4.

◆§ SOY CHEESE SOUFFLE

2 tbs. oil
2 tbs. whole wheat flour
1 cup milk (soy or dairy)
½ cup tofu

½ cup uncooked soy grits
¾ tsp. salt
4 eggs, separated

Blend oil and flour, and add milk. Cook over low flame until thick. Add soy cheese and stir. Add dry soy grits and salt. Pour this mixture into beaten egg yolks and fold into stiffly beaten whites. Pour into greased casserole and bake in pan of hot water and moderate oven until mixture sets, or about 1 hour. Serve hot. Serves 4.

✒ TOFU IN SOUP

Steamed strips or pieces of tofu may be added to any soup in place of noodles. Cook tofu and add to hot soup before serving.

✒ TOFU SANDWICH SPREAD

Mash raw or cooked tofu, add desired amount of salt, powdered vegetable broth, and other seasonings. Mix well and use as sandwich spread on bread or crackers. Minced chives, ripe olives, or pimiento are good additions.

( )
( )

SOY CEREALS AND BREAKFAST DISHES

There are any number of excellent ready-to-cook and ready-to-eat soy cereals on the market. They range from sweetened all-soy grits to mixtures fortified with only a small amount of soy. Soy grits, plain or puffed, may be used as 100 percent soybean mush or cereal, or they may be added to any other cereal to provide extra protein. The most popular cereals are those made of grains with a small amount of soy meal or soy grits added. The starch content, of course, is higher in this type of cereal, which should be noted for the low-starch diet.

Most soy cereals are excellent not only in food value but also in taste. The soybean adds a nutlike flavor. Soy cereals may be eaten with dairy milk or cream or with soy milk, and served with fresh fruit or berries. Soy cereals may be added to muffins, hot cakes, waffles, and cookies, and they may also be made into puddings. Directions for these dishes are usually given on the package.

Cereal Recipes

◆§ MIXED CEREAL

1 lb. steel-cut oats
1 lb. soy grits
1 lb. rye grits
1 lb. cracked whole wheat

Mix all together. Store in jar or tin and use as needed. Cook as whole wheat cereal 20 to 30 minutes with three times as much water as cereal. Salt to taste. This mixture may be toasted in oven before cooking.

◆§ SOY WHEAT CEREAL

Mix equal parts fine cracked wheat and soy grits. Cook as whole wheat cereal.

◆§ SOY WHEAT GERM CEREAL

1 lb. wheat germ
1 lb. medium or fine soy grits

Mix. Cook in 2 qts. salted water for 5 minutes. Many doctors suggest this combination as a high-protein and low-starch cereal.

◆§ SOY, WHEAT, AND WHEAT GERM CEREAL

1 lb. fine cracked wheat
1 lb. wheat germ
1 lb. fine soy grits

Mix all together. Cook 20 minutes in 2 qts. or more salted water.

✍ WHEATLESS CEREALS

These are used for wheat-allergy diets and may be mixed as desired. A few combinations are these, mixed in equal parts:

    Steel-cut oats, soy grits
    Coarse corn meal, soy grits
    Steel-cut oats, corn meal, soy grits
    Rye grits, barley grits, soy grits
    Rye grits, barley grits, steel-cut oats, corn meal, soy grits

Cook as for regular cereal.

Soy Breakfast Dish Recipes

✍ GRANOLA

    1 cup wheat flour (soft or hard)
    ½ cup barley flour
    1 cup millet flour
    1 cup soy flour
    ½ cup white or brown rice flour
    ½ cup rye flour
    1 tbs. salt
    3 tbs. sesame seed
    ½ cup oil
    ½ cup honey
    ½ cup water
    1 cup oatmeal
    ½ cup corn meal

Mix together flours, salt, and sesame seed. Then add oil, honey, and water, and mix into granules. Bake in moderate oven until nicely browned, stirring occasionally. Then turn fire out and let dextrinize in oven, stirring several times after fire is turned off. Store in airtight container. Serve with milk (soy or dairy), or fruit. Serves 8 to 10.

❧ SESAME TOAST 1

Lightly toast soy bread. Spread with thin layer of margarine and turn upside down on plate of sesame seeds. A thin coating of sesame seed will stick to bread. Put under broiler for toasting. You won't have to urge your family for seconds on this toast!

❧ SESAME TOAST 2

Toast soy bread under broiler on one side. Brush untoasted side lightly with water and turn upside down on plate of sesame seeds. Put sesame side up under broiler until nicely browned. Watch carefully as sesame seeds will burn quickly.

❧ SOY FRENCH TOAST

    1 cup soy milk
    ¼ cup cashew nuts
    ¼ cup sunflower seeds
    ¼ tsp. yeast extract
     Salt to taste
     Soy or whole wheat bread

Liquefy first four ingredients. Remove from liquefier and salt to taste. Dip bread in this mixture and brown lightly in oil or brown in hot oven. If you do not have a liquefier, you may substitute cashew butter and sunflower seed meal.

As variations, a smoked flavor or vegetable chicken flavor may be used in place of yeast extract; and other nuts may be substituted for cashews and sesame seed for sunflower seeds.

◆§ SOY WAFFLES

1 cup soy milk
¼ cup soy flour
¾ cup whole wheat flour
1 tbs. oil
1 tsp. salt
1 tbs. brown sugar

Mix thoroughly and bake in hot waffle iron until nicely brown. These waffles rise by steam and take a few minutes longer than other types of waffles. Serves 1 or 2.

As variations, any combination of flour equaling 1 cup may be used, for example, all corn meal or corn flour, corn and soy flour, all rye, or all buckwheat.

◆§ SOY GRITS PANCAKES

2 eggs
1 cup buttermilk
½ tsp. salt
1 cup uncooked medium or fine soy grits

Separate eggs. Beat yolks until fluffy and light, whites until stiff. Add buttermilk, salt, and grits to yolks. Allow mixture to stand a few minutes to allow grits to soften; then fold in egg whites. Bake as pancakes on hot griddle. Cakes will be a little thick and are crunchy. Serve with vegetables and/or gravy or tomato sauce. Serves 2.

For more meatlike flavor, add a small amount of soy sauce or food yeast.

◆§ SWEET MILK PANCAKES

    ½ cup soy flour
    1½ cup whole wheat flour
    2 tsp. brown sugar
    ½ tsp. salt
    2 eggs, separated
    1¾ cups milk
    2 tbs. oil or melted shortening

To sifted dry ingredients, add mixture of well-beaten egg yolks, milk, and shortening. Fold in stiffly beaten egg whites. Bake as small cakes on hot griddle.

◆§ CORN MEAL AND SOY PANCAKES
(No Wheat)

    2 eggs, separated
    1¾ cups soy milk
    1 cup corn meal
    ½ tsp. salt
    2 tbs. oil

Beat egg yolks until frothy and whites until stiff. Add milk to yolks. Sift dry ingredients, add milk and egg yolk mixture, and lastly add oil. Fold in egg whites lightly. Bake on heavy griddle. Serves 2 to 3.

SOY GRIDDLE CAKES

These can be used in place of meat, fish, or other protein dishes.

    2 eggs, separated
    ½ tsp. salt
    1 to 1¼ cups soy flour
    1 cup soy milk

Beat egg yolks, and add milk. Sift soy flour with salt. The amount of flour depends on the size of the eggs and how thick you wish the batter. Stir liquid into dry mixture. Fold in egg whites, beaten stiff. Bake on hot, heavy griddle with as little fat as possible. If sweetening is desired, add 1 tsp. honey.

SOY
DESSERTS

Delicious and nutritious desserts can be made from soy bread, soy grits, and soy cereals. Soy milk desserts are often called for in allergy cases, but they also make a fine addition to a normal diet. Soy milk may be used in place of regular milk in any prepared and packaged puddings.

Soy Pudding and Other Dessert Recipes

❧ SOY BREAD PUDDING

1 cup soy milk
1 cup prune juice
2 cups soy bread, cubed
1 egg, or ⅓ cup cashew butter
1 cup cooked prunes, chopped
1 tsp. lemon extract

Pour milk and prune juice over bread cubes. Add beaten egg, prunes, and extract. Bake in oiled casserole in moderate oven 45 minutes. Serve hot or cold, with rich soy milk or soy topping. Serves 6.

✊§ CARROT FRUIT PUDDING

- 2 eggs, or ½ cup cashew butter
- 2 cups cooked carrots, mashed
- 2 cups chopped dates, or 1 cup chopped dates and 1 cup raisins
- 1 cup apple juice
- 2 cups soy cookie crumbs or breadcrumbs
- ¼ tsp. salt

Beat eggs and add rest of ingredients. Mix well. Bake in oiled casserole in moderate oven 30 minutes. This pudding may be baked in individual custard cups. Serve hot or cold, with soy or other favorite topping. Serves 4 to 6.

✊§ SOY DATE PUDDING

- 2 eggs, or ½ cup cashew butter
- 1 cup soy milk
- 2 tbs. honey
- 2 tbs. oil
- 1 cup dates, chopped or ground
- 1 cup soy Melba toast crumbs
- 1 tsp. lemon juice, or 1 tbs. orange juice
- Pinch of salt

Beat eggs; add soy milk, honey, oil, dates, crumbs, and flavoring. Mix well. Pour into oiled baking dish and bake

30 minutes in moderate oven. Serve with custard sauce.
Serves 4.

◄§ SOY PUMPKIN PUDDING

6 tbs. honey
½ cup whole wheat pastry flour
¼ tsp. salt
1 cup cooked pumpkin
1 tsp. vanilla
1½ cups soy milk

Blend together and bake in moderate oven for 45 minutes. Individual molds may be used. Pudding is delicious topped with orange sauce:

2½ tbs. cornstarch
Pinch of salt
1⅓ cups hot water
½ cup frozen concentrated orange juice

Cook together until thick. Chill before serving.

◄§ SOY APPLE BETTY

4 cups whole wheat breadcrumbs
½ cup soy grits mixed with ½ cup water
½ cup brown sugar
½ tsp. salt
4 cups diced apple
1 tbs. oil

Mix breadcrumbs and soaked soy grits. Mix sugar and salt.
Place a layer of the crumb and soy grits mixture in oiled
baking dish or casserole. Top with layer of diced apple.

Sprinkle with sugar mixture. Repeat layers until casserole is full. Top with crumbs, and sprinkle with oil. Cover and bake until apples are soft, about 30 to 45 minutes. Remove cover toward end of baking and allow crumbs to brown. Dates or raisins may be added. Serves 4 to 5.

◆§ SOY CEREAL PUDDING

- 1 cup leftover cooked soy cereal
- ½ cup brown or raw sugar
- 2 eggs beaten lightly, or ½ cup soy or almond butter
- 2 cups milk (soy or dairy)
- ½ cup chopped dates or raisins

Mix thoroughly. Pour in greased baking dish, and top with sprinkling of breadcrumbs and brown sugar. Bake in moderate oven 20 minutes. Serve with cream or pudding sauce. Serves 4.

◆§ SOY GRITS PUDDING

- ¾ cup uncooked soy grits
- 1½ cups water
- ½ tsp. salt
- 4 tbs. brown sugar
- 2 tbs. molasses
- ½ cup seedless raisins
- 2 eggs
- 1 cup soy milk
- 1 tsp. maple flavoring

Add grits to boiling salted water. Cook 3 to 5 minutes, or until dry. Add sugar, molasses, and raisins. Mix well. Beat eggs; add milk, grits mixture, and maple flavoring. Pour into oiled casserole and bake in moderate oven for 1¼ hours. Serve with soy cream. Serves 4.

◅§ SOY BUTTERSCOTCH PUDDING

      4 tbs. brown sugar
      4 tbs. cornstarch
     ¼ tsp. salt
     1½ cups soy milk
     ¾ cup dark corn syrup or mild honey
      2 egg yolks
      2 tbs. margarine

Mix sugar, cornstarch, and salt in saucepan. Gradually add milk, then syrup, and mix well. Cook, stirring constantly until mixture thickens. Beat egg yolks slightly, and blend in cooked mixture a little at a time. Continue cooking for 5 minutes. Remove from heat, add margarine, and pour into individual dessert dishes. Top with soy cream. Serves 4.

Egg yolks may be omitted by liquefying ¾ cup cashews with the soy milk.

◅§ CREAMY RICE PUDDING

     ½ cup uncooked rice
      5 cups liquid soy milk
      1 tsp. salt
     ⅓ cup brown sugar
      2 tsp. corn oil
     Vanilla to taste

Wash rice and drain. Add milk and salt, and pour into oiled baking pan or casserole. Cook over fire, stirring often, until rice begins to float. (It is the stirring that gives it the creamy consistency.) Add sugar, oil, and vanilla. Mix well, and set in slow oven. Cook until rice is thoroughly done and top slightly browned. Remove and cool. Serves 6.

⋘ HEAVENLY RICE

  2 cups cold cooked brown rice
  ½ cup pitted dates, chopped
  1 or 2 tbs. honey
  ½ cup nuts, coarsely chopped
  1 cup pineapple, crushed or tidbits
  1 cup soy whip topping

Mix ingredients and chill thoroughly. Garnish with any kind of fruit or berries, fresh or frozen. Serves 4 to 6.

⋘ RICE WITH SOY MILK

  ½ cup uncooked brown rice
  2 cups soy milk
  4 tbs. honey
  ¼ cup raisins
  ½ tsp. salt

Wash rice, add to soy milk, and cook over flame until mixture begins to boil. Then add honey, raisins, and salt. Cook in double boiler until milk is absorbed and rice is done, or bake in covered casserole for 40 minutes in moderate oven. Serves 4.

⇜§ COCONUT TOFU

  1 cup mashed tofu
  1 cup grated fresh coconut
  4 tbs. honey
  1 tsp. vanilla

Mix all together, chill, and serve, topped with toasted coconut or chopped nuts. Serves 2 or 3.

⇜§ SOY CUSTARD

  2 eggs
  2 cups soy milk
  ¼ tsp. salt
  2 tbs. molasses
  2 tsp. vanilla

Beat eggs slightly; add milk, salt, molasses, and vanilla. Stir well. Pour into small baking dish or casserole. Set in pan of hot water. Bake in moderate oven for about 1 hour, or until a silver knife inserted in custard comes out clean. For chocolate-flavored custard, add 2 tsp. carob powder and use only 1 tsp. vanilla. Serves 4.

⇜§ BLANCMANGE

  2 cups soy milk
  3 tbs. sugar or honey
  ⅛ tsp. salt
  4 tbs. cornstarch
  Vanilla or any desired flavor to taste

Put milk into double boiler, and when boiling hot, add sugar and salt. Blend cornstarch with a little cold milk and pour gradually into hot milk, stirring constantly. Cover and let cook 15 minutes. Add vanilla or other flavoring. Turn into individual molds or a large mold. Serve unmolded with lemon or carob sauce. Serves 4.

⋙ INDIAN PUDDING

  1 qt. soy milk
  ¼ cup corn meal
  ¼ cup sugar
  ½ cup molasses
  1 tbs. corn oil
  1 tsp. salt

Scald milk in double boiler. Add corn meal slowly, while stirring, and cook 20 minutes. Add remaining ingredients. Turn into oiled 1½-qt. casserole, and bake uncovered in slow oven about 3 hours, stirring once during baking. Serve either hot or cold. Serves 6.

This pudding can be baked in advance and then reheated in slow oven.

⋙ CAROB PUDDING

  3 tbs. cornstarch
  4 tbs. brown sugar
  2 tbs. soy flour
  3 tbs. carob powder
  ¼ tsp. salt
  2 cups soy milk
  2 tsp. vanilla

Mix cornstarch, sugar, soy flour, carob, and salt. Gradually add milk and blend thoroughly. Cook, stirring constantly,

3 or 4 minutes or until mixture is thick. Remove from flame, add vanilla, pour into molds or dessert dishes, and cool. Serve with soy cream. Serves 4.

Soy Ice Cream

Soy milk may be used in place of milk in ice cream recipes. Follow regular directions, substituting soy milk for milk and adding whipped cream. Part dairy and part soy milk may be used if desired.

The best way to make ice cream is in an old-fashioned ice cream freezer, turned by hand or by motor. This makes the smoothest ice cream, and the following recipes will be creamy and have a fine texture if made in this way. They may be made in the freezing compartment of the refrigerator, but they should be whipped once or twice while freezing.

✒ VANILLA ICE CREAM

¼ cup corn oil
½ cup honey
1 tbs. vanilla
Dash of salt
1 cup soy milk powder
2½ cups water

Place all in liquefier and whiz. Freeze in hand freezer. Makes 1 qt.

This can be varied by adding fruit, nuts, and different flavors.

∝§ MAPLE NUT ICE CREAM

- ½ cup maple syrup
- 1 tbs. maple flavoring
- 2 tbs. vanilla
- 2 cups soy milk powder mixed with 6 cups water
- 1 cup nuts, chopped

Mix all except nuts in liquefier. Add nuts and freeze in hand freezer. Makes 2½ qts.

∝§ ORANGE ICE CREAM

Dissolve 1 pkg. orange vegetable gelatin in 2 cups boiling water. Add 3 cups orange juice or 1 can frozen orange juice made up. Whiz in liquefier the following:

- 1 cup soy milk powder
- ½ cup honey
- ½ cup oil
- 3 cups water
- 1 tbs. orange flavoring

Mix all together and freeze in hand freezer. Makes 2½ qts.

∝§ STRAWBERRY ICE CREAM

- 3 boxes (1½ qts.) fresh strawberries
- 5¾ cups water
- ¾ cup honey
- ¾ cup oil
- 2 cups soy milk powder
- Dash salt

Whiz all except strawberries in liquefier. Then add strawberries and freeze in hand freezer. Makes 3¾ qts.

⊷§ SOY FRUIT ICE CREAM

  1 banana
  1 cup brown sugar or honey
  Juice of 1 orange
  Juice of 1 lemon
  Pinch of salt
  1 cup soy milk
  1 cup coconut milk

Mash banana; add sugar, fruit juice, and salt. Blend with soy and coconut milk. Coconut milk may be made from fresh coconut or coconut powder by adding water. Freeze mixture in hand freezer. May be topped with chopped nuts before serving. Makes 2 qts.

If made in refrigerator, whip several times while freezing.

⊷§ SOY TOPPING

    1 cup water
    1 cup soy milk powder (malt or all-purpose)
 ½-¾ cup oil
 ½-¾ tsp. vanilla
  5-6 drops lemon juice

Mix water with soy milk powder in liquefier or blender. Add vanilla, then add oil gradually until mixture is the consistency of whipped cream. Add lemon juice and chill.

Note: 1 tsp. lecithin (granules or liquid) will make a smoother, creamier mixture and will allow you to use a little less oil.

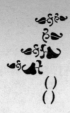

SOY
CANDIES

There are several so-called soy chocolates on the market containing soy flour or soy powder. Most of them resemble ordinary milk chocolate and may be used for beverages, candy, baking, and frostings. Specialty food stores now carry a product containing carob and soy and no chocolate, that looks and tastes like milk chocolate.

Soy Candy Recipes

DIPPED SOY CAROB CANDIES

Nuts, dates, and dried fruits may be dipped in soy carob candy. Melt a small amount of carob candy over hot water. When soft, dip fruits or nuts in it and place them on wax paper to harden. Ground dried fruits, such as figs or raisins, may be shaped into balls and dipped. Nut-stuffed dates are delicious when dipped. Raisins, nuts, or ready-to-eat cereal may be mixed into melted carob candy and dropped by spoonful on wax paper as clusters.

✠§ SOY CRUNCHES

Melt a small amount of soy carob candy. Add enough ground toasted soybeans to take up candy and yet stick together. Drop as clusters on wax paper to harden.

✠§ SOY DELIGHT

Many stores sell candy on this order—a white or chocolate divinity containing soy flour or soy milk powder.

    2 cups granulated sugar
    ½ cup hot water
    ½ cup corn syrup
    2 egg whites
    Pinch of salt
    4 tbs. unsweetened powdered soy milk
    ½ tsp. vanilla

Mix sugar, water, and corn syrup, and boil together until hard ball forms when a drop is tested in cold water. Beat egg whites with pinch of salt until stiff and dry. Pour hot syrup gradually into egg whites, beating constantly. Add powdered soy milk and vanilla and continue beating until stiff. Pour into buttered pan to cool. Cut into squares.

Nuts or ground toasted soybeans may be added if desired. Carol powder may be added while heating.

⋖§ SOY PANOCHA

   3 cups brown sugar
   ½ cup corn syrup
   ⅔ cup water
   2 egg whites
   4 tbs. powdered soy milk
   1 cup ground toasted soybeans or nuts

Boil sugar, corn syrup, and water until a hard ball forms when a drop is tested in cold water. Beat egg whites dry; pour hot syrup in gradually. Add powdered soy milk. Beat constantly until mixture thickens. Add ground toasted soybeans. Shape into balls, or pour into buttered pan and cut into squares.

⋖§ SOY CAROB FUDGE

   2 cups brown sugar
   4 tbs. carob
   ⅓ cup water
   ⅓ cup soy milk
   1 cup toasted soybean flour
   1 tbs. corn syrup or honey
   2 tbs. margarine
   1 tsp. vanilla
   Nuts if desired

Blend sugar and carob. Mix water and milk with soy flour and add to sugar and carob. Mix well. Add syrup and cook to 230° or medium-soft-ball stage. Stir constantly when cooking. Remove from fire; add margarine. Allow mixture to cool, add vanilla and nuts, and beat until thick. Pour into buttered pan. When cold cut into squares.

❧ SOY CAROB FUDGE (Uncooked)

¼ cup vegetable butter
½ cup honey
½ cup carob powder
½ cup nuts
¾ to 1 cup soy milk powder
1 tsp. vanilla
  Cereal crumbs or chopped nuts

Cream honey and butter, and add other ingredients. Shape into logs about 6″ long. Roll in crumbs or chopped nuts. Refrigerate. Slice as needed.

( )
( )

SOY FLOUR
BREADS

Soy flour is creamy in color, fluffy, and fascinating to work with. It is not a flour as are grain or potato flours, but is more on the order of powdered milk and powdered eggs in use and in concentration of food value. Using soy flour is an easy and economical way of stepping up the protein content of any baked product.

Since soy flour does not contain gluten or starch, it cannot be used by itself in ordinary recipes and must be mixed with other flours. A small amount may be added to bread, biscuits, muffins, pancakes and waffles, pastries, cakes, and cookies. Soy flour bakery products stay fresh longer, toast better, and have a delicate nutlike flavor.

Full-Fat Soy Flour   Full-fat flour is simply the ground-up soybean, with nothing removed and nothing added. It may be ground raw, in which case the product has an un-palatable raw bean flavor and odor, or it may be toasted or processed in some way to remove the bean flavor.

Low-Fat or Fat-Free Soy Flour This flour has had part or all of the fat removed. Usually the raw bean flavor has been processed out. This product is sometimes sold under the trade name of soy powder.

How to Use Soy Flour

A mixture of 2 tablespoons of soy flour with every cup of wheat flour can be used in practically every recipe. More soy, even as much as 50 percent, can be used if desired, especially in muffins, waffles, pancakes, and quick breads. Muffins can be made with all soy flour, but they will not be light and will have a definite soy taste.

Soy flour browns easily and requires careful baking. Do not have the oven too hot. It is always wise to lower the oven temperature at least 25° for baking when adding soy flour to an ordinary recipe.

Soy-flour products require a little more salt or flavoring than do other flour products. An extra amount of added water or liquid is usually necessary also if a high percentage of soy flour is used.

Always sift soy flour before measuring.

Bread Roll, and Muffin Recipes

You may use 10 to 30 percent soy flour in any bread recipe. Beat in some wheat flour before adding the soy flour. Fresh or dry yeast may be used; 1 package of dry yeast equals 1 cake of fresh yeast or 1 tablespoon of bulk dry yeast.

A secret of good bread is never to chill the dough. Keep it warm and away from drafts, and keep it covered with a towel. For good texture, an even temperature all the way through is important—heat the flour, bowl, pans, etc. Heating the flour also cuts the rising time. Always knead the dough well.

For soft crusts on bread, brush the loaf or rolls with oil as soon as removed from the oven.

⋘§ SOY GLUTEN BREAD

    1 yeast cake dissolved in ¼ cup lukewarm water
    1 cup water and 1 cup soy milk, or 2 cups soy milk
    1 tbs. oil
    1 tsp. salt
    1 tsp. brown sugar
    1 cup gluten flour
    2 cups soy flour
    3 cups white flour

Break yeast cake into lukewarm water. Heat 1 cup water, pour into bowl, and add oil. Add cold milk, salt, sugar, and yeast. Add gluten flour, 1 cup soy flour, and 1 cup white flour. Beat until smooth and full of air bubbles. Add 1 cup soy flour and about 2 cups white flour, or enough to make a stiff dough. Knead thoroughly, adding flour on board until dough does not stick to hands or board. Place in oiled bowl, cover, and let rise until double in bulk. Punch down and let rise again. Remove from bowl and shape into 2 loaves. Place in oiled pans, cover, and let rise until almost double in bulk. Bake in moderate oven 1 hour.

✑ SOY BREAD

    3 tbs. oil
    ½ cup brown sugar or honey
    1½ tsp. salt
    2 cups soy milk, scalded
    1 cake yeast dissolved in ½ cup warm water
    7 cups flour, of which ¼ soy flour

Add oil, sugar, and salt to scalded milk. Let cool. Add dissolved yeast cake and work in flour to make a medium-stiff dough. Knead well. Let rise. Knead again and shape into loaves. When bulk has doubled, bake in moderate oven. Care must be taken that crust does not burn, because this bread browns very quickly.

For rolls, add 1 or 2 eggs to above recipe and 1 more tbs. oil. Follow directions for bread, and bake ½ hour or more in moderate oven. 1 to 2 tbs. liquid lecithin may be substituted for eggs.

✑ SOY GLUTEN ROLLS

Follow the above recipe, shaping dough into rolls instead of loaves. Place rolls close together in oiled pan, cover, and let rise until double in bulk. Bake in moderate oven 20 to 30 minutes, depending on size. Brush with oil when removed from oven.

✑ QUICK WHOLE WHEAT BREAD

This recipe makes good-textured and -flavored loaves that cut without crumbling, and can be made in 1½ hours.

    1½ cups of hot water
    2 tsp. salt

6 tbs. honey
2 tbs. soybean oil
1 pkg. dry yeast dissolved in ½ cup warm water
5 cups whole wheat bread flour

Place hot water, salt, honey, and oil in a large bowl. Cool.
Add dissolved yeast. Beat in 3 cups warm flour, or enough
to make a stiff batter. Cover and set in warm place 15 minutes. Add about 1½ cups warm flour and knead until
dough is not sticky, adding flour as necessary. Shape into
loaves or biscuits and put in well-oiled pans.

Place loaves and/or biscuits in a cold oven set at 250°
(f.) for 15 or 20 minutes. While oven is heating it acts as
a proof box and bread will rise. After 15 or 20 minutes,
turn oven up to about 350° to finish baking. Large loaves
will take 45 to 50 minutes, smaller loaves and rolls less
time to finish baking. When done, remove bread from
pans, oil top, and cool on rack before slicing. Makes 2
large loaves or 3 small loaves. We like the small loaves
best.

This bread may be made with soy milk or with half water and half soy milk or potato water. Wheat germ may be
added. Molasses may be used instead of honey.

⊷§ WHOLE WHEAT SOY BREAD 1

Follow the above recipe, using

4 cups whole wheat bread flour
1 cup soy flour

Beat in 2 cups whole wheat flour; add soy flour. Mix and
let rise. This makes 2 loaves of 20 percent soy bread. Less
soy flour may be used if desired.

Note: You may use this quick method where a longer

method is given in your favorite recipe or in any of the
bread recipes in this chapter.

◦§ WHOLE WHEAT SOY BREAD 2

   1 cake fresh yeast dissolved in 1 cup lukewarm water
3½ tsp. honey
   1 cup soy flour
   3 cups whole wheat flour
½ cup lukewarm soy milk
   1 tsp. salt
1½ tbs. oil

Break yeast into water. Add ½ tsp. honey. Let mixture
stand until it bubbles. Beat in ¾ cup soy flour and ½ cup
whole wheat flour. This will make a soft sponge. Let stand
until light. Then add soy milk, salt, 3 tsp. honey, and oil.
Mix well and add to sponge. Beat in ¼ cup soy flour and
2¼ cups whole wheat flour. This will make a dough stiff
enough to knead. Remove to floured board and knead
with a light touch. Add whatever flour is necessary so
that dough will not stick to hands or board. Shape in ball
and place in deep oiled bowl. Let rise until double. Punch
down and let rise again. Shape into loaves. This will make
1 very large loaf, 2 small, or 1 medium loaf and a few
buns. Let rise until almost double. Bake in moderate oven
1¼ hours (longer if one large loaf).

◦§ WHOLE WHEAT SOY ROLLS

   1 cake fresh yeast dissolved in ¼ cup lukewarm water
   1 tbs. honey
   1 tsp. salt

1¼ cups lukewarm soy milk
2 tbs. oil
3 cups whole wheat pastry flour
1 cup soy flour

Break yeast cake into lukewarm water with 1 tbs. honey. For sweeter rolls, add more honey. Let stand until bubbly. Add salt, soy milk, and oil. Beat in 1 cup whole wheat pastry flour and soy flour. Let rise until light and add about 2 cups whole wheat pastry flour. Knead and place in oiled bowl. Let rise until double in bulk, punch down, let rise again, and shape into rolls. For high biscuits, make round balls and place close together. For buns, place farther apart. May be made as Parker House rolls, twists, or cloverleaf, place 3 small balls in buttered muffin tin, let stand until double in bulk. Bake in moderate oven at least 30 minutes.

These rolls may also be made like cinnamon rolls with raisins. Roll into strips, oil inside, add raisins, and coil into biscuit shape. Place close together in pan, let rise, and bake.

৶ SPROUTED WHEAT BREAD

2 tbs. yeast (2 pkgs.) dissolved in 1 cup lukewarm water
¼ cup honey
2 cups warm water
3 tbs. oil
½ cup soy flour
5 cups whole wheat bread flour
1 tbs. salt
2 cups sprouted wheat, ground twice in food chopper (made by same method as sprouted soy beans)

Put dissolved yeast and honey into a large mixing bowl. Let stand until yeast is growing—about 10 minutes. Add water, oil, soy flour, 3 cups whole wheat flour, and salt. Beat until elastic, and put in warm place to rise until about double in bulk. Add sprouted wheat. Work mass into sponge. Then work in 2 cups whole wheat flour. Knead until dough is smooth and elastic. Make into loaves, and put into cool oven 15 minutes. Turn oven up to moderate heat and finish baking—about 1 hour, depending on size of loaf. Cool on wire rack out of pan. Makes 3 loaves.

⋐§ EZEKIEL'S BREAD (Pumpernickel Texture)

> 1 cup warm water
> 3 tbs. honey or brown sugar
> 2 tbs. yeast (2 pkgs.)
> 1 cup hot water
> 1½ tbs. salt
> 1 cup sprouted or soaked lentils
> 3 tbs. oil
> 2 cups hot water
> 1 cup soy flour
> 1 cup rye flour
> 1 cup gluten flour
> 1 cup millet flour
> 1 cup barley flour
> 4 cups whole wheat bread flour

Mix warm water, 1 tbs. honey, and yeast and let stand until yeast is growing well. Liquefy together 1 cup hot water, 2 tbs. honey, salt, lentils, and oil until smooth, and put in large bowl. If no liquefier is available, put lentils through food mill twice. To lentil mixture, add 2 cups hot water and first five flours. Beat thoroughly and add yeast mixture. Beat again and add 1 cup whole wheat flour. Allow to stand in warm place 15 minutes. Then add about 3 cups whole wheat flour, enough to make a dough easy to handle but not too stiff. Knead for 6 or 8 minutes. Make into loaves or rolls and put into cool oven. Allow 15 minutes for bread to rise; increase oven temperature to moderate, and finish baking (approximately 1 hour; less for rolls and small loaves). Makes 4 or 5 loaves.

∾§ CORN BREAD

½ cup dry soybeans soaked overnight, or 1⅓ cups soaked soybeans
2 tbs. oil
1 tsp. honey or brown sugar
2 tbs. sesame seeds (optional)
1 tsp. salt
2 cups water
1½ cups corn meal

Liquefy soybeans, oil, honey, sesame seeds, and salt with part of water. Remove from liquefier to bowl, and add remaining water. Add corn meal and mix thoroughly. Bake in oiled corn-stick pans or square pan 45 minutes in moderate to high oven.

∾§ OPEN-RECIPE BREAD

This loaf of bread is made according to the open recipe sponsored by the Emergency Food Commission of New York State and developed by the School of Nutrition at Cornell University. The recipe is designed to produce a loaf of bread unusually high in nutritive value. The original recipe called for enriched unbleached wheat flour with added wheat germ, high-fat soy flour, dry skim milk, sugar, yeast, pure lard, salt, and sufficient water to prepare. If you wish to make this same distinctive, highly nutritious bread at home, simply follow any standard directions for making bread and use these ingredients for a 2-loaf batch:

> 6 cups sifted enriched, unbleached flour with added wheat germ
> 1 cake yeast
> 3½ tbs. powdered soy milk
> 2 cups water
> 3 tsp. salt
> 2½ tsp. honey
> 9 tbs. high-fat soybean flour
> 1⅓ tbs. oil

2¼ cups fluid soy milk may be used in place of the milk powder and water listed above.

⊷§ SOY COFFEE CAKE

> 1 yeast cake dissolved in 4 tbs. lukewarm water
> 1 cup soy milk
> 3 tbs. oil
> 3 tbs. sugar or honey
> ½ tsp. salt
> 1 cup soy flour
> 3 cups white flour
> 1 egg, or 1 tbs. liquid lecithin
> 3 tbs. brown sugar mixed with chopped nuts

Break yeast cake into water and let stand a few minutes. Heat milk until lukewarm, pour into mixing bowl, and add oil, sugar, and salt. Stir and add dissolved yeast, ½ cup soy flour, and 1 cup white flour. Cover mixture and let stand until it bubbles; then add beaten egg, ½ cup soy flour, and about 2 cups flour. Mix well and knead as for bread. Place dough in oiled bowl and let rise until double in bulk. Remove from bowl and knead slightly. Flatten with rolling pin and shape into loaf about 1″ thick. Place in well-oiled cake pan, cover, and let rise until double in bulk. Brush top with melted butter, and top with brown sugar and nuts. Bake 30 minutes in moderate oven.

✑ SOY WHOLE WHEAT COFFEE CAKE

Follow above recipe using whole wheat pastry flour instead of white flour. Whole wheat pastry flour may also be used for sweet rolls and fancy twists.

✑ FANCY TWISTS

Use coffee cake recipe. When dough is double in bulk, knead slightly and break off small portions. Roll thin and shape into coils or figure eights. Dip into sugar. Place in oiled pan and let rise until double. Bake 15 to 20 minutes in moderate oven. Honey may be used for glaze instead of sugar.

✑ SOY MELBA TOAST

Soy Melba toast may be purchased or made at home. An entire loaf may be made at one time, and the toast may be stored in an airtight container. If using unsliced loaf, do not slice too thin. Place slices of soy bread in slow oven and bake until golden brown. Bread will brown quickly. Be sure to turn slices if necessary to brown evenly.

✑ REFRIGERATOR ROLLS

    ½ cup water
    1 tsp. salt
    4 tbs. sugar or honey
    6 tbs. shortening or oil
    ½ cup soy milk
    1 yeast cake dissolved in 3 tbs. lukewarm water
    1 egg, or 1 tbs. liquid lecithin
    ½ cup soy flour
    3½ cups white flour

Heat water. Add salt, sugar, shortening, and milk. Stir until shortening is melted. Add yeast, well-beaten egg, soy flour, and 1 cup white flour. Beat well. Add rest of flour, enough to make a dough stiff enough to knead. Place on floured board and knead several minutes. Place ball of dough in greased bowl, brush with oil, cover, and store in refrigerator. For rolls, remove amount of dough desired. Shape into small balls and place in greased baking pan. Cover and let rise until double in bulk. Bake in moderate oven about 15 minutes, or until nicely browned.

✑ DATE NUT BREAD

    2 tbs. shortening or oil
    1 cup brown sugar
    1 cup dates, chopped
    ½ cup nut meats
    1 tsp. salt
    1 cup white flour or enough to make a thick batter
    1 cup soy flour
    1 pkg. yeast dissolved in 2 tbs. lukewarm water
    1 cup soy milk

Cream shortening and sugar. Add nut meats and dates, salt, sifted flours, dissolved yeast, and soy milk. Beat. Pour into oiled loaf pan. Let rise ½ hour in warm place. Bake in slow oven 1 hour.

✑ DATE RING

Use your favorite bread recipe. Take a piece of dough the size of your two fists. Roll out into rectangle about ⅓″ thick. Spread with date butter or any ground fruit. Nuts may be added if desired. Roll up like jelly roll. Shape like crescent on oiled cookie sheet. Make slits with a knife every 2″ or 3″ on the outside. Allow to rise until double, or place in cool oven for 15 or 20 minutes, and then turn oven up to moderate for 30 minutes or so, until done and nicely brown.

✑ FRUIT NUT BREAD

   ½ cup soy flour
 1½ cups white flour
   1 pkg. dry yeast
   ½ tsp. salt
   2 tbs. shortening or oil
   ½ cup brown sugar
   1 egg, or 1 tbs. liquid lecithin
   ¾ cup soy milk
   ½ cup dates, chopped
   ½ cup raisins
   ½ cup nut meats
   1 tsp. orange rind, grated

Sift flours separately. Measure, and sift with yeast and salt. Cream shortening and sugar; add beaten egg, milk, fruit, and nut meats. Mix well; add orange rind and dry ingredients. Beat. Place in well-oiled loaf pan, and bake in moderate oven about 1 hour.

⊷ SOY NUT BREAD

    1 cake compressed or dry yeast
    1 cup lukewarm water
    3 cups white flour
    1 cup soy flour
 1½ tsp. salt
   ¼ cup brown sugar or honey
    1 egg, or 1 tbs. liquid lecithin
    2 tbs. oil
   ½ cup raisins
    2 cups walnuts, chopped

Dissolve yeast in water. Stir into this ½ the flour. Set in warm place. When light, stir in remaining ingredients, and knead until dough is smooth. It is much easier to mix this with a bread mixer. Make into small loaves and put into cool oven for 15 or 20 minutes. Turn oven up to moderate and finish baking—about 30 to 40 minutes more.

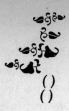

( )
( )

PASTRY

These tender, flaky pie crusts may be used for your favorite cream pie filling or for any fruit pie. Double the single-shell recipes to make two-crust pies.

In these recipes, you may use half white flour and half whole wheat bread flour if you do not have whole wheat pastry flour. Always use a third as much shortening as flour, and do not cut the shortening into the flour too much; larger particles of shortening give a flakier crust.

Pie Crust Recipes

✦§ SOY PIE CRUST 1

    1 cup white flour
    2 tbs. soy flour
    ½ tsp. salt
    6 tbs. vegetable shortening
    Enough cold water to make dough

Sift flours and salt. Cut in shortening. Add water to make a smooth ball. Place on well-floured board, and cover with sheet of oiled paper. Roll thin. Line pie tin with dough and bake in moderate oven until brown. Makes 1 large pie shell.

☙ SOY PIE CRUST 2

⅓ cup soy flour
⅔ cup white flour
½ tsp. salt
5 tbs. shortening
3 to 4 tbs. cold water

Sift flours and salt. Cut in shortening. Add enough water to make a smooth ball. Place on floured board and roll thin. Line pie plate with dough and bake in moderate oven until brown. Makes 1 pie shell.

☙ SOY PIE CRUST 3

1 cup soybean flour
1½ cups white flour
1 tsp. salt
5 or 6 tbs. fat
2 to 3 tbs. cold water

Sift flours and salt. Work in fat with tips of fingers or a fork or biscuit cutter. When flour and fat are grainy, add water slowly, using no more than absolutely necessary to make a stiff dough. Proceed as above. Makes 2 crusts.

⋖§ SOY WHOLE WHEAT PIE CRUST 1

Follow recipe for Soy Pie Crust 2, using

1 cup whole wheat pastry flour
2 tbs. soy flour

⋖§ SOY WHOLE WHEAT PIE CRUST 2

½ cup whole wheat pastry flour
½ cup soy flour
½ tsp. salt
4 tbs. shortening
4 tbs. cold water

Sift flours and salt, and cut in shortening. When well blended, add minimum cold water needed. Place dough on floured board and roll as thin as possible. Bake in moderate oven until brown. Makes 1 large pie crust.

⋖§ STIR 'N' ROLL PIE CRUST

⅓ cup soy oil
3 tbs. cold water or milk
1⅓ cups whole wheat pastry flour
1 tsp. salt

Pour oil and water or milk over flour and salt. Mix just enough to hold together. Roll between 2 sheets wax paper, and put into 9″ pie pan. Bake 12 to 15 minutes in medium-hot oven. Cool and add filling.

If desired, 2 tbs. soy flour may be substituted for 2 tbs whole wheat flour.

◦§ CEREAL PIE CRUST

2 cups prepared soy cereal, crumbled fine
2 tbs. whole wheat flour
⅛ lb. margarine
1 tbs. honey

Mix together and press firmly into bottom and sides of 9-inch pie pan. Bake in medium-hot oven 8 to 10 minutes. Cool in refrigerator. May be used in place of graham cracker crust.

Pie Filling Recipes

◦§ BANANA CREAM PIE

Use recipe for Blancmange, omitting 1 tsp. cornstarch. Put layer of banana in bottom of crust, which may be whole wheat or cereal shell. Pour in layer of pudding; add layer of banana. Alternate until all pudding is used. Top with soy topping or whipped cream.

As a variation, coconut cream pie can be made the same way; either mix coconut right into blancmange, or put it in layers. Use favorite topping.

Carob candy may be melted and dripped over layers of blancmange.

◦§ LEMON CHIFFON PIE

1 pkg. vegetable gelatin, lemon-flavored
1½ cups water
1 cup canned dairy milk, chilled

1 tsp. lemon juice
1 tsp. lemon rind, grated

Make vegetable gelatin according to directions, using 1½
cups water. Cool. While cooling, whip canned milk; then
mix in vegetable gelatin, lemon juice, and rind, and pour
into baked pie shell.

᥍ PUMPKIN PIE

Scant ½ cup sugar
4 tbs. browned flour
1½ cups cooked pumpkin
1 tbs. molasses
⅛ tsp. salt
½ tsp. vanilla
1½ cups double-strength soy milk, hot

Mix sugar with browned flour, and add to pumpkin. Combine all ingredients and blend well. Pour into unbaked pie
crust and bake in medium oven until set and a light brown
color.

( )
( )

COOKIES

Soy flour may be used in any favorite cookie recipe to make an enriched or more nourishing cookie. The amount of soy flour used will vary according to taste and recipe. Whole wheat pastry flour may be used with the soy in your favorite cookie recipes.

Soy Cookie Recipes

✒ SOY COOKIES

3½ heaping tbs. white flour
1 tbs. soy flour
1¼ tbs. sugar
4 tbs. oil
A little soy or dairy milk if too stiff

Cream all together and force through pastry tube in fancy shapes onto well-greased baking sheet. Bake in hot oven

10 minutes. Let cool on baking sheet before removing to cookie jar. Makes about 1 dozen.

⊷ GROUND SOYBEAN WAFERS (No Flour)

These cookies are crisp and delicious, and are welcomed by those who cannot have cereal flours.

    2 eggs
    1 cup brown sugar
    1 tsp. vanilla
    3 cups toasted soybeans, ground

Beat eggs until thick and lemon-colored. Add sugar and vanilla. Grind beans in food chopper, using fine knife, and add to above mixture. No salt is added because beans are salty. This will make a stiff dough. Drop by teaspoonful onto oiled cookie sheet, and pat to ¼″ thickness with fork dipped in water. Bake in moderate oven until brown. Remove at once from pan. Makes about 4 dozen.

⊷ HEALTH COOKIES

    1 cup oil
    1 cup brown sugar
    2 eggs
    1 cup chopped raisins or other dried fruit
    3 cups oatmeal
    1 cup soy flour
    1 cup whole wheat pastry flour
    ¼ tsp. salt
    4 tbs. soy milk

Cream shortening and sugar; add beaten eggs and raisins. Add oatmeal and sifted flours with salt. Add milk, and mix well. This will be a stiff dough. Drop with teaspoon on oiled cookie sheet, flatten with fork, and bake in moderate oven until brown. Makes about 2 dozen.

✑ SOY DATE BARS

  2 eggs, separated
  1 cup brown or raw sugar
  4 tbs. boiling water
  1 cup walnuts, chopped
  1 cup dates, chopped
  1 tsp. vanilla
  1 cup whole wheat pastry flour
  ½ cup soy flour
  ½ tsp. salt

Beat egg yolks, add sugar and water, and continue beating until lemon-colored. Add nuts, dates, and vanilla. Sift in flours and salt. Mix well; then fold in stiffly beaten egg whites. Bake in shallow, well-oiled pan in moderate oven about 35 minutes. Cut in squares or strips. Makes about 4 dozen.

✑ FIG ROCKS

  3 eggs
  1½ cups brown sugar
  1 cup oil
  2 cups black figs, ground
  1 cup walnut meats (optional)
  ½ cup warm water
  1 tsp. vanilla
  1½ cups whole wheat pastry flour
  1 cup soy flour

Beat eggs well; add to sugar and oil. Add ground fruit and nut meats, and mix well. Add water, and last add flours. Drop by spoonsful onto oiled tin, and bake in moderate oven until brown. Makes about 5 dozen.

As variations, 1 cup raisins and 1 cup figs may be used.

ᕯ FRUIT DROPS

    1¼ cups soy flour
    ¼ cup whole wheat pastry flour
    ½ tsp. salt
    2 eggs, separated
    ¼ cup honey
    ½ cup soy cream
    1 cup raisins or dates, chopped
    1 tsp. vanilla

Sift flour several times. Add salt. Beat egg yolks, and add. Add honey, cream, raisins, and vanilla. Fold in flour and mix well. Fold in beaten egg whites. Drop by spoonsful onto oiled cookie sheet, and bake in moderate oven until brown. Makes about 3 dozen.

ᕯ SUGAR COOKIES

    ½ cup shortening
    1 cup brown sugar
    1 egg, beaten
    ½ cup milk
    ½ cup soy flour
    2 cups white or whole wheat pastry flour
    ½ tsp. salt
    ½ tsp. vanilla

Cream sugar and shortening. Add beaten egg; add alternately milk with other ingredients sifted together. Add vanilla. Roll to ¼″ thickness on floured board, sprinkle with white or brown sugar, and cut into cookies. Bake on oiled cookie sheet in moderate oven until brown. Makes 4 dozen.

❧ PEANUT BUTTER COOKIES 1

  ½ cup oil
  1 cup brown sugar
  1 egg, well beaten
  ½ cup peanut butter
  1 tsp. vanilla
  ¼ tsp. salt
  ¼ cup soy flour
  1¼ cups whole wheat pastry flour

Add oil and sugar to egg. Beat; add peanut butter and vanilla. Sift in salt and soy flour. Add whole wheat flour and mix well. Drop by teaspoonsful onto oiled cookie tin and bake in moderate oven until brown. Makes about 3 dozen.

❧ PEANUT BUTTER COOKIES 2

  ½ cup oil
  1 cup brown sugar
  2 eggs, well beaten
  ½ cup peanut butter
  ¼ cup water
  2 cups whole wheat pastry flour
  ½ cup soy flour
  ½ tsp. salt

Whip oil; add sugar and eggs. Add peanut butter, water, and dry ingredients. Mix well. Drop by teaspoonsful onto oiled cookie sheet; flatten with a fork. Bake in moderate oven until brown. Makes about 4 dozen.

⋖§ WHEAT GERM WAFERS

½ cup oil
1 cup brown sugar
1 egg
4 tbs. milk
2 tsp. vanilla
½ cup whole wheat pastry flour
½ cup soy flour
¼ tsp. salt
½ cup wheat germ

Pour oil over sugar and let stand a few minutes. Add well-beaten egg, milk, and vanilla, and fold in sifted flours with salt. Add wheat germ. Drop by teaspoonsful onto well-oiled cookie sheet. If egg is large, batter may be a little thin, and more wheat germ should be added. Bake in moderate oven until brown. Makes about 2 dozen.

A small amount of coconut is a good addition.

⋖§ ICEBOX COOKIES

2 eggs
½ cup oil
2 cups brown sugar
3 cups whole wheat pastry flour, or 1½ cup whole wheat and 1½ cup white flour
½ cup soy flour
½ tsp. cream of tartar

½ tsp. salt
½ cup nut meats
½ tsp. vanilla

Beat eggs well; add to creamed oil and sugar. Mix well. Add 1 cup flour with cream of tartar and salt. Add nuts, vanilla, and rest of flour. Knead dough if necessary. Shape into roll and chill in refrigerator for several hours. Slice into thin cookies and bake in moderate oven until brown. Makes about 5 dozen.

⊷ WHEAT GERM ICEBOX COOKIES

½ cup oil
1 cup brown sugar
1 egg, separated
3 tbs. soy milk or orange juice
1 tsp. vanilla
½ tsp. salt
1 cup wheat germ
1½ cups whole wheat pastry flour
½ cup soy flour

Cream oil and sugar; add well-beaten egg yolk, milk or orange juice, vanilla, salt, and wheat germ. Work in sifted flours. This will make a stiff dough. Blend thoroughly, shape into a roll, wrap in wax paper, and chill in refrigerator overnight. Slice and bake in moderate oven until brown. Makes about 3 dozen.

৵ SOY CRUNCH COOKIES

  1 cup oil
  1 cup brown sugar
  2 eggs
  4 tbs. soy milk
  1 tsp. almond extract
  ½ cup whole wheat pastry flour
  2 cups ground toasted soybeans or nuts
2½ cups oatmeal

Cream oil and sugar. Add beaten eggs, milk, and extract.
Fold in sifted flour. Add ground soybeans and oatmeal.
Mix well. Drop by teaspoonsful onto oiled cookie sheet;
flatten with fork dipped in cold water. Bake in moderate
oven. Makes about 3 dozen.

These may be made without any flour, using 2½ cups
ground soybeans. They are delicious, but break very easily.

৵ BRITTLE COOKIES

¾ cup brown sugar
1 tbs. oil
1 tbs. water
½ tsp. salt
⅓ cup soy flour
⅓ cup ground toasted soybeans

Mix sugar, oil, and water, together. Add salt, flour, and
soybeans. Drop with spoon on well-greased sheet. Bake in
slow oven until brown. Remove at once from pan. May
be rolled over stick if handled while warm. Makes about
2 dozen.

◆§ SOY BROWNIES

  1 cup brown sugar
½ cup oil
  1 tsp. vanilla
  1 egg, separated
¼ tsp. salt
¼ cup soy flour
¼ cup white flour
  2 tbs. carob powder
½ cup nuts, chopped

Cream sugar and oil, and then add vanilla and beaten egg
yolk. Add salt, flours, carob powder, and nuts. Fold in egg
white, beaten until stiff; then put into oiled and flour-
dusted square pan. Bake 20 minutes in moderate oven.
Remove from pan, cut, and cool. Makes about 2 dozen.

◆§ MOLASSES BROWNIES

½ cup oil
½ cup brown sugar
½ cup molasses
  2 tbs. carob powder
  1 egg
½ cup whole wheat pastry flour
½ cup soy flour
¼ tsp. salt
  1 cup nuts, chopped

Cream oil and sugar; add molasses, carob, and well-beaten
egg. Sift in dry ingredients, and add nuts last. Pour into
shallow, well-oiled pan and bake in a slow oven 40 to 45
minutes. Cut in squares. Makes about 2 dozen.

✑ MOLASSES THINS

   1 egg
   1 cup brown sugar
   ¾ cup oil
   ¼ cup molasses
   ¼ tsp. salt
   ½ cup soy flour
   2 cups whole wheat pastry flour

Beat egg; add sugar and oil. Add molasses. Sift in salt and soy flour. Add whole wheat flour and mix well. Shape into rolls, wrap in wax paper, and chill several hours in refrigerator. Slice thin and bake until brown in moderate oven. Makes about 3 dozen.

✑ HONEY MOLASSES CHEWS

   ½ cup honey
   1 cup oil
   1 tsp. vanilla
   Grated rind of two medium oranges
   1 cup oat flour or ground oatmeal
   ½ cup molasses
   1 cup fine macaroon coconut
   1 scant tsp. salt
   1 cup soy flour
   2 cups whole wheat pastry flour

Combine first 8 ingredients and mix well. Add sifted flour, 1 cup at a time, and mix thoroughly. Drop by spoonsful onto greased cookie sheet. Bake in moderate oven until brown. Makes about 2 dozen.

◅§ WHOLE WHEAT AND OAT STICKS

- ⅔ to 1 cup soy milk
- ½ to ⅔ cup oil
- 1 tsp. salt
- ½ cup coconut, grated
- ½ cup sesame seeds, lightly toasted (optional)
- 3 tbs. honey
- ⅔ cup nuts, ground
- 2 cups dates, cut in half and pitted
- 2 cups whole wheat flour
- 2 cups oat flour

Add enough soy milk to other ingredients to make a dough to roll. Divide dough and roll out in greased pans to ⅛" thickness. Prick with fork and cut in strips about 1" wide and about 3" long. Bake in hot oven until brown. Watch edges, as it may be necessary to take out some sticks before the whole pan is browned. Makes about 4 dozen.

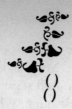

( )
( )

CAKES

A small amount of soy flour can be added to many cake recipes with excellent results. It is especially fine in spice and fruit cakes. Use your favorite recipe.

Soy Cake Recipes

◆§ SOY HEALTH CAKE

    1 cup white flour
   ¾ cup soy flour
    2 heaping tbs. cornstarch
    4 large eggs, or 5 small eggs, separated
   ½ cup water
 1¾ cups sugar
   ½ cup oil
   ¼ tsp. salt
   Vanilla or other flavoring

Sift flour before measuring. Then measure, and sift with cornstarch at least six times. Beat yolks and water until light and foamy and rather thick. Add sugar and beat as you add. Then add oil, salt, and flavoring. Whip together until oil is taken up (not too vigorously). Put flour in all at one time. Fold in beaten egg whites. Bake in slow oven about ½ hour; then increase heat to moderate and bake ¾ to 1 hour more.

◁§ FRUIT CAKE 1

- ¼ lb. citron peel
- ¼ lb. orange peel
- ¼ lb. raisins
- ½ lb. pineapple and cherries
- ½ cup grape juice
- 1 cup walnuts, chopped
- ¼ lb. margarine or shortening
- ½ cup honey
- 3 eggs, separated
- ½ cup white or whole wheat pastry flour
- ½ cup soy flour
- ½ tsp. salt

Cut up fruit, mix, and place in bowl. Cover with grape juice, let stand overnight, and add nuts. Cream shortening. Add to it honey, then beaten egg yolks, and soaked fruit; last, fold in flour, sifted several times with salt. Mix well; add stiffly beaten egg whites, and pour mixture into buttered loaf pan. Bake 1¼ to 1½ hours in moderate oven.

◆§ FRUIT CAKE 2

½ cup oil
1 cup dark brown sugar
Few drops almond flavoring
1 tsp. vanilla
½ tbs. lemon flavoring
1 lemon rind, grated
½ tsp. salt
1 cup applesauce, hot and unsweetened
2 cups pastry flour
2 tbs. soy flour
2 pkgs. dry yeast dissolved in ½ cup warm water
1 cup nuts, whole or large broken pieces
1 cup ea. of following dried or candied fruits, chopped and dredged in a little flour: pineapple, cherries, orange peel, raisins, dates, prunes or dried figs

Blend oil and sugar, adding flavoring, a little salt, and hot applesauce. Mix well and add part of flour to cool mixture. Add yeast, nuts, and remainder of flour, and pour over cut-up fruit. Mix lightly but thoroughly. Place in oiled and floured tube or loaf pan. Allow to rise in warm place until light. Bake 1 hour in moderate oven. Let set overnight (it's better next day). Cut with sharp knife after several hours in refrigerator.

◆§ APPLESAUCE CAKE

1 cup shortening
2 cups brown sugar
2 eggs, separated
1½ cups thick applesauce, unsweetened
1 cup soy flour

2½ cups whole wheat pastry flour
 1 tsp. salt

Cream shortening and sugar. Add beaten egg yolks and applesauce. Sift dry ingredients and stir into sugar mixture; add stiffly beaten egg whites. Bake in shallow loaf or deep layer-cake tin for 40 to 50 minutes in moderate oven. For small cake, cut recipe in half.

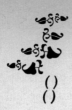

EXTRA
TIPS

Soy-Enriched Meat Dishes

Soy grits, regular or puffed, and soy flour may be used to stretch a meat loaf, patties, sausages, and stews. The addition of soy products greatly increases the protein content and lessens the loss of juices in frying as much as 15 percent. Additional water is always necessary, and additional seasoning is advisable.

◆§ REGULAR GRITS WITH MEAT

Soak grits in water or cook as cereal. Use ⅓ cup cooked or soaked soy grits to ⅔ cup ground meat. Mix well, blending the grits thoroughly into the meat. Then follow a regular recipe for a loaf, patty, or sausage. Less grits may be used or as much as ½ cup grits to ½ cup ground meat.

✎§ PUFFED SOY WITH MEAT

Use 1 pound ground beef, 1 cup puffed soy grits, and ½ cup liquid. Mix, and follow a regular recipe.

✎§ SOY FLOUR WITH MEAT

Use 1 pound lean ground beef, ½ cup soy flour, and ½ cup liquid. Mix the flour with the meat, add liquid, and follow a regular recipe. More or less soy flour may be used with the proper amount of liquid.

( )
( )

APPENDIX

Browned flour—made by lightly browning wheat flour in oven or on top of stove in dry pan. It must be watched carefully to avoid burning. This process gives a delicious nutlike flavor to any dish where flour is used.

Carob candy—made from carob powder, and very similar to milk chocolate. It may be purchased as such and used in cookies, or it may be melted like regular chocolate and used as coating for fruits and nuts.

Carob powder—a chocolatelike brown powder made by finely grinding the carob pod which grows on a tree belonging to the locust family. It is used as a chocolate replacement in the recipes in this book.

Coconut cream—may be purchased fresh or in cans in most specialty food shops. It may be made at home by liquefying 1 cup unsweetened coconut with 2 cups warm water for 3 to 5 minutes. Then strain and discard pulp.

Coriander seed—may be purchased whole or powdered. It is usually used in cookies and desserts.

Cumin or cuminos—ground seed, used in chili and curry powder. Purchased in any spice department.

Double-strength soy milk—or rich soy milk—made by using more soy milk powder than the directions call for.

Gluten products—any of the commercially made vegetable protein foods made largely from the protein part of wheat, which is known as gluten.

Herb seasoning—many of the more commonly used, non-irritating herbs are included in these recipes. They may be purchased in any spice department, and may be had in powdered or dry leaf form. The powdered herbs are much more concentrated than the leaf, therefore, use about ½ as much.

Italian seasoning—a combination of herbs used in Italian dishes.

Liquid lecethin—often used in the baking industry as an extender of fat or as a replacement of eggs to make a product smoother (not as a leavening agent). It may be purchased at a bakery or specialty food shop. It looks thick and dark, like molasses or dark honey.

Long rice or bean thread—may be purchased at any Oriental store. If you don't have it or can't get it, you may substitute fine soy noodles or spaghetti.

McKay's vegetable chicken seasoning—is the trade name of a vegetable mock-chicken seasoning. It is sold in all specialty food shops. If not obtainable, George Washington Golden Broth, sold in nearly all general markets, may be substituted.

Meat tenderizers—sold under many trade names in spice departments. They are made largely of papain powder and may be purchased with or without spice.

M.S.G. or monosodium glutamate—seasoning made from vegetable protein. It is the sodium salt of one of the amino acids. In this book it is abbreviated M.S.G. It may be purchased in any spice department under many trade names or as M.S.G. It has been used in the Orient for generations, and was used in this country commercially for many years before it was offered to the retail trade.

Papain powder—the digestive enzyme from the tropical papaya melon. It may be purchased in pure form from a specialty food shop or as a meat tenderizer from the general market.

Powdered vegetable broth—mixed powdered vegetables in combination for broth, with or without salt and onions. Adds a delicious flavor to many dishes.

Rich soy milk—see double-strength soy milk.

Salad herbs—a combination of various herbs that go well in salad; sold under this name.

Smoked meat flavor—there are several such products on the market, and all are vegetable unless otherwise labeled. They usually contain yeast or soy powder.

Soy sauce—also called bean juice. Made from a water extraction of soybeans, it may be purchased in any general market. It is a very concentrated salty liquid and must be used sparingly.

Tahini—sesame butter. Sold in all specialty food stores.

Tumeric—a yellow coloring made from the root of an herb. Purchase in a spice department.

Vegetable burger—a ground gluten (wheat protein) product that is made commercially and sold under various trade names. It can be used in any recipe where ground meat is used.

Vegetable gelatin—made from plants and/or vegetable pectins or gums and sold at specialty food stores under several trade names. Make according to directions on package.

Vegetable protein foods—made commercially from a number of vegetable proteins, which are formulated in such a way as to serve as very palatable as well as nutritious replacements for animal protein. They come in the form of cutlets or steaklets, or are ground to resemble hamburger. Many of these products contain wheat gluten, which gives them a chewy texture not unlike the texture of meat.

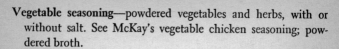

Vegetable seasoning—powdered vegetables and herbs, with or without salt. See McKay's vegetable chicken seasoning; powdered broth.

Vegetable stock—vegetable broth seasoned with vegetable chicken flavoring or yeast extract. May be used anywhere a meat or chicken broth is required.

Whole wheat pastry flour—finely ground soft wheat flour used in making pastry, cookies, cake, etc. It contains less protein than bread flour and therefore will not make good bread; however, it makes light, flaky pastry.

Yeast

    Baker's yeast—the kind used in making bread. It is live yeast.

    Brewer's yeast—a by-product of the brewery industry. The yeast plant has been destroyed, so it is no longer alive. It is a highly concentrated form of protein and vitamins, particularly the B complex.

    Food yeast—grown primarily as a food supplement. It has more protein and a better balance of vitamins than brewers' yeast; however, the big difference is in the flavor. It is much milder, and gives a delicious flavor where used.

Yogurt—thick cultured milk made by adding yogurt culture to warm soy or dairy milk, allowing it to stay in a warm place until the desired thickness, and then refrigerating.

Menus

ᏬᏘ MONDAY

BREAKFAST

Fruit or Juice
Soft-Cooked Egg
Toasted Whole Wheat Soy Bread   p. 184
Milk or other beverage

LUNCH

Potato Soy Cheese Salad   p. 117
Refrigerator Rolls   p. 192
Fresh Fruit with Tofu   p. 142
Beverage

AFTER SCHOOL SNACK

Soy Shakes   p. 141
Health Cookies   p. 201

DINNER

Onion Soup with Croutons and Parmesan
    Cheese   p. 108
Bean Sprout Creole   p. 58 (or Meat Loaf with
    Tomato Sauce)
Broccoli
Green Soy and Cucumber Salad   p. 38
Apple Betty   p. 168
Beverage

TUESDAY

BREAKFAST

Fruit Juice
Puffed Soy Grits with Cream p. 26
Hot Whole Wheat Muffins—Honey p. 182
Milk or other beverage

LUNCH

Puree of Soybean Soup—Cheese Wafers p. 107
Molded Salad p. 38
Fresh Fruit
Beverage

AFTER SCHOOL SNACK

Apple, Peanut Butter Cookies p. 204

DINNER

Tomato Juice Cocktail—Melba Toast p. 191
Chow Mein with Rice p. 59
Soy Fruit Ice Cream p. 176
Beverage

☙ WEDNESDAY

BREAKFAST

Vegetable Juice
Scrambled Eggs and Soy Puffs   p. 84
Whole Wheat Toast
Milk or other beverage

LUNCH

Sandwiches—Soy Olive Spread   p. 126
Green Salad—Honey dressing   p. 120
Beverage

AFTER SCHOOL SNACK

Milk, Molasses Brownies   p. 208

DINNER

Fresh Fruit Cup
Soy Eggplant Patties   p. 83 (or Hamburger Patties)
Green Peas
Baked Potatoes
Whole-Wheat Bread   p. 184
Heavenly Rice   p. 171
Beverage

ৎও THURSDAY

BREAKFAST

>Fruit or Fruit Juice
>Buttermilk Pancakes—Honey   p. 163
>Milk or other beverage

LUNCH

>Tossed Salad   p. 56
>Ezekiel's Bread   p. 188
>Soy Butterscotch Pudding   p. 170
>Molasses Thins   p. 209
>Beverage

AFTER SCHOOL SNACK

>Milk and Fruit Nut Bread   p. 193

DINNER

>Consomme
>Meatless Chili Con Carne   p. 88
>Hot Tortillas (wrapped in napkin)
>Shredded Lettuce (as side dish)
>Fresh Fruit Gelatin
>Beverage

FRIDAY

BREAKFAST

> Sliced Orange or ½ Grapefruit
> Puffed Soy Grits with Cream   p. 26
> Milk or other beverage

LUNCH

> Soy Grit Vegetable Soup   p. 109
> Toasted Gluten Bread   p. 183
> Apple Pie—Soy Pie Crust   p. 195
> Sharp Cheddar Cheese
> Beverage

AFTER SCHOOL SNACK

> Milk and Banana

DINNER

> Jellied Madrilene
> Broiled Mackerel
> Boiled Potatoes
> Stuffed Tomatoes   p. 76
> Refrigerator Rolls   p. 192
> Strawberry Short Cake

⋙ SATURDAY

BREAKFAST

Melon or other Fresh Fruit
Coddled Eggs
Toasted Soy Bread   p. 184
Milk or other beverage

LUNCH

Cream of Tomato Soup   p. 109
Whole Wheat Bread Sandwiches   p. 185
with Soy Butter Filling   p. 130
Applesauce
Beverage

DINNER

Bouillon, Melba Toast   p. 191
Soy and Mushroom Loaf   p. 67 (or Broiled
   Lamb Chops)
Fresh Spinach
Baked Potatoes
Waldorf Salad   p. 115
Health Cake   p. 211
Beverage

⋖§ SUNDAY

BREAKFAST

 Sliced Oranges
 Waffles   p. 163
 Honey or Maple Syrup
 Milk or other beverage

LUNCH

 Cream of Pea Soup   p. 110
 Corn Bread   p. 189
 Fresh Fruit Salad, Cottage Cheese
 Beverage

DINNER

 Consomme
 Soy Melba Toast   p. 191
 Soy Loaf   p. 65 (or Roast Chicken)
 Asparagus
 Succotash   p. 35
 Green Salad with Mayonnaise   p. 121
 Apple Dumplings
 Beverage

() ()

INDEX

arco Books
on Health and Nutrition

VITAMIN E
Your Key to a Healthy Heart

Herbert Bailey

WHY IS VITAMIN E therapy for mankind's foremost killing disease still controversial in the United States? This is one of the questions asked and answered in this slashing, fully-documented book. It tells how the efficacy of vitamin E in the treatment of cardiovascular disease was discovered by Dr. Evan Shute of Canada, and of the remarkable cures effected by him and his brother, also a doctor . . . how the author himself suffered a severe heart attack and how in a short time he was restored to normal active life by massive doses of the vitamin . . . how a barrier against vitamin E has been erected in this country by the medical traditionalists of the American Medical Association at the same time that it is being widely used with spectacular results in such medically-advanced countries as England, Germany, France, Italy, and Russia . . . how continuing study indicates that vitamin E may be an effective preventive for diabetes, sterility, arthritis and a variety of other diseases. "Literally worth its weight in gold."
—The Pittsburgh Courier   **$1.65**

GET WELL NATURALLY

Linda Clark

LINDA CLARK believes that relieving human suffering and obtaining optimum health should be mankind's major goal. She insists that it does not matter whether a remedy is orthodox or unorthodox, currently praised or currently scorned in medical circles—as long as it works for you. Miss Clark, who is also the author of **Stay Young Longer**, makes a plea for the natural methods of treating disease—methods which do not rely on either drugs or surgery. Drawing not only from well-known sources but also from folklore and from the more revolutionary modern theories, she presents a wealth of information about diseases ranging from alcoholism to ulcers. Here are frank discussions of such controversial modes of treatment as herbal medicine, auto-therapy, homeopathy, and human electronics, plus some startling facts and theories about nutrition and about the natural ways of treating twenty-two of the most serious illnesses that plague modern man.   **$1.65**

FOOD FACTS AND FALLACIES
Carlton Fredericks and Herbert Bailey

A noted nutritionist and veteran medical reporter present medical evidence based on modern research to prove that a good diet can lessen your effects of coming down with one of today's common health problems, such as heart disease, arthritis, mental illness, and many others. This book gives the unadulterated facts about fad diets, and it presents some startling information about proper diet and the prevention and treatment of alcoholism. To help you be sure that you are getting the balanced meals you need, the authors have included eleven rules for menu selection; tips on buying meats, cereals, and breads; lists of common sources of vitamins, carbohydrates, and fats; and an appendix of suggested menus. **$1.45**

LOW BLOOD SUGAR AND YOUR HEALTH
Eat Your Way Out of Fatigue
Clement G. Martin, M.D.

In this revolutionary new book, Dr. Martin tells exactly how to determine if hypoglycemia is the cause of fatigue problems, and if so, he outlines a diet that can make anyone feel better after the first week. It's not a starvation diet, not a fad diet. But it is unusual. The Doctor instructs the reader to eat eight times a day rather than three. And for those who don't suffer from hypoglycemia, it is still probable that the cause of the fatigue or mental distress is nutrition. These people will find Dr. Martin's delicious, eight-times-a-day diet pouring new energy into their bodies.

This is not a book of "miracle cures." It is a book about common sense attitudes toward nutrition and exercise—proof positive that a sensible, well-balanced diet is the **real** key to good health. **$1.65**

ARCO BOOK OF ORGANIC GARDENING

Joseph A. Cocannouer

A blueprint for soil management designed to enable you to grow better-testing, healthful, fruits, vegetables and other food crops. Here is complete information on **organic** gardening and farming—gardening without poisonous pesticides—where to start, what to do and how to follow through whether in a window box, backyard or on acres of soil. Everything you need to know to make friends with the earth the natural way is included—organic soil conditioners, composts and mulches, pest control without poison, tips on planting and landscaping.
Clothbound: $4.50
Paperbound: $1.45

NATURE'S MIRACLE MEDICINE CHEST

C. Edward Burtis

How to achieve abundant good health through everyday wonder foods—pure natural foods, our gifts from the land and sea. Mr. Burtis covers many of the wonder foods found in nature's miracle medicine chest and explains how to use them for better health—the fantastic papaya melon, digestive disorders and the lime, slipped discs and vitamin C, cabbage juice and ulcers, yogurt and digestive health, calcium and the heart, bone meal and loose teeth, garlic and diarrhea, the bactericidal qualities of honey, the remarkable powers of royal jelly, kelp for the common cold, cod liver oil and arthritis, vitamin E and the heart, brewer's yeast as a protective agent, sesame seeds as a tranquilizer.
Clothbound, $5.95

COMMON AND UNCOMMON USES OF HERBS FOR HEALTHFUL LIVING

Richard Lucas

A fascinating account of the herbal remedies used through the ages. Plant medicine has been used for thousands of years and modern science is now re-evaluating many old-time herbal medicines. Described here are the herbal folk remedies that have been used for centuries by the American Indians, the gypsies, the ancient herbalists, the countryfolk, and the old-time country doctor. The background, history and uses of such healing herbs as dandelion, elder, nettle, sage, kelp, onion, parsley, sassafras, rosemary, camomile, corn silk, celery as cures for rash, hives, urinary disorders, ulcers, gout, and nervous disorders are described. $1.65

HEALTH, FITNESS, and MEDICINE BOOKS